The
AMERICAN
ENVIRONMENTAL
MOVEMENT

In 1990, the 20th anniversary of Earth Day spawned festive
public events and made environmentalists ask themselves,
"How far have we come?" Most answered, "Not far enough."
(S.C. Delaney, Environmental Protection Agency)

■SOCIAL REFORM■
M O V E M E N T S

The
AMERICAN
ENVIRONMENTAL
MOVEMENT

REBECCA STEFOFF

Facts On File®

AN INFOBASE HOLDINGS COMPANY

The American Environmental Movement

Copyright © 1995 by Rebecca Stefoff

Facts On File, Inc.
460 Park Avenue South
New York, NY 10016

Library of Congress Cataloging-in-Publication Data

Stefoff, Rebecca, 1951–
    The American environmental movement / Rebecca Stefoff
       p. cm. — (Social reform movements)
    Includes bibliographical references and index.
    ISBN 0-8160-3046-4 (alk. paper)
    1. Environmentalism—United States—Juvenile Literature. 2. Earth Day—United States—Juvenile Literature. [1. Environmental protection.] I. Title. II. Series.
    GE195.5.S74 1995
    363.7'0525'0973—dc20   94-33393

Facts On File books are available at special discounts when purchased in bulk quantities for businesses, associations, institutions or sales promotions. Please contact our Special Sales Department in New York at 212/683-2244 or 800/322-8755.

Text design by Fred Pusterla
Cover design by Nora Wertz

Printed in the United States of America

MP FOF   10 9 8 7 6 5 4 3 2 1

This book is printed on acid-free paper.

C O N T E N T S

ACKNOWLEDGMENTS

The author would like to thank the following people and organizations for their contributions to this book: Professor Edward O. Wilson of the Museum of Comparative Zoology, Harvard University; Mike Morgan and the National Zoological Park, Smithsonian Institution; Nancy Roswurm and the U.S. Department of Agriculture Forest Service Office in Portland, Oregon; the Wilderness Society; Steve Delany and the Environmental Protection Agency; the Citizens Clearinghouse for Hazardous Waste; and Captain Paul Watson, Lisa Distefano and Celia Alario, of the Sea Shepherd Conservation Society.

P R O L O G U E

The First Earth Day

Fourth-grade students from the Sacred Heart School in New York City did not start the day in their classrooms as usual on Wednesday, April 22, 1970. Instead they went to Union Square in downtown Manhattan and started sprucing up the scruffy park with brooms, shovels, and rakes donated by the city's electric company. While they were working, John Lindsay, the mayor of New York, dropped by to offer encouragement. He even wielded a broom for a few minutes. For the girls from Sacred Heart, this was definitely not an ordinary school day. They were getting Union Square ready for what was later called "the largest organized demonstration in human history"—the first Earth Day.

Union Square was only one of thousands of places around the United States where Earth Day was celebrated. On the other side of the country, in Washington State, where the deep, cool waters of Puget Sound are bordered by a wide, multilane freeway, a hundred high school students from Tacoma climbed into the saddle and took Earth Day on the road. To the astonishment of motorists, the students rode horses down the freeway in a stunt designed to call attention to the air pollution caused by automobiles.

Cars were targeted in other parts of the country that day. Students in Danbury, Connecticut performed a solemn burial service: To show that they wanted the age of fossil fuels and pollution to end, they buried a car's engine. Students at Michigan's Wayne State University picketed outside the offices of General Motors, the automobile manufacturer. Cars were banned altogether from a 45-block stretch of Fifth Avenue in New York City and from part of Miami, Florida. To remind people of alternatives to cars, Earth Day demonstrators rode everything from buses to bikes to skates to hot-air balloons.

Earth Day was an event dedicated to the environment: to the air, water, sea, and land, and to the creatures of Earth. It was a day of education, of celebration, and of protest. For some participants, Earth Day was "an ecological carnival" or "an exuberant rite of spring." Other people used Earth Day to call attention to abuses of the environment, such as litter, air and water pollution, and toxic waste. There were plenty of demonstrations and speeches about these and other issues across the land. The U.S. Congress was in recess for the day because so many of its members had seized the chance to make public appearances. In the nation's capital, 10,000 people gathered at the Washington Monument for a rally that combined a rock concert with speeches expressing concern for the environment. Larger crowds gathered at rallies and street fairs in other cities; as many as 100,000 people passed through New York's Union Square, hub of that city's Earth Day activities, and events in Philadelphia, Chicago, and San Francisco drew 25,000 people.

Above all, however, Earth Day was intended to be a day for teaching and learning about the environment, and most of those who took part in it were students. More than 10,000 schools and 2,000 colleges and universities arranged special classes for the day. In Philadelphia, the seven days leading up to April 22 were set aside as Earth Week, with environmental events and classes all week long in the schools.

The world's first large-scale oil spill had occurred just a few years before Earth Day, in 1967, when the *Torrey Canyon* spilled 37 million gallons of oil into the sea off the coast of Britain. The memory of the spill was still strong in 1970 and was reflected in several Earth Day events. In Ridgefield, Connecticut, students poured oil into tanks of water to create miniature oil spills and observed how the oil moved across the water and coated everything it touched. In San Francisco, a band of activists calling themselves "Environmental Vigilantes" dumped oil into a decorative pool outside the office building of Standard Oil of California to protest the oil slicks that had been caused at sea by petroleum drilling and shipping operations.

In a style of protest that has been labeled "guerrilla theater," activist groups like the Environmental Vigilantes carried out several dramatic public protests. Students at the University of Illinois

Girl Scouts remove old tires and other debris from the Potomac River in Washington, D.C. on Earth Day, 1970. Since the first Earth Day, cleanups have become an annual event on many of the nation's waterways and beaches. *(Library of Congress)*

disrupted a speech by a spokesperson for an electric company by coming up onto the stage, throwing soot on each other, and coughing to show the effects of air pollution from the company's smokestacks. In Florida, protesters delivered a dead octopus to another power company, this one accused of discharging destructive heat into local waters.

Stunts like these grabbed the headlines, but the vast majority of Earth Day activities were quietly constructive. In hundreds of locations, classroom groups and troops of Boy Scouts and Girl Scouts picked up litter from beaches and parks, gathered aluminum cans and newspapers for recycling, or weatherproofed the homes of elderly people to help them save energy. According to the National Education Association, about 10 million children in public schools took part in Earth Day classes or field trips. Several million more people participated in the events on college campuses and in urban rallies. Earth Day was nationwide in scope and included a broad array of viewpoints and issues. The day was hailed by the *New York Times* as "the first mass consideration of the globe's environmental problems."

Many historians of the American environmental movement regard Earth Day 1970 as the birth of modern environmentalism. But it is more accurate to think of the first Earth Day as the day environmentalism came of age. Earth Day gave new purpose and direction to a movement that had been growing for many years. On April 22, 1970, concern for the environment emerged as a true American mass movement, one that was supported by a substantial portion of the public. The roots of that movement, however, can be traced far back into America's past.

PROLOGUE NOTES

p. vii   "the largest organized demonstration . . ." Attributed to Denis Hayes, Earth Day organizer, in *Philip Shabecoff,* **A Fierce Green Fire: The American Environmental Movement,** p. 113.

p. viii   "ecological carnival . . . exuberant rite . . ." **New York Times,** April 23, 1970, p. 1.

p. x   "the first mass consideration . . ." **New York Times,** April 23, 1970, p. 1.

The
AMERICAN
ENVIRONMENTAL
MOVEMENT

CHAPTER One

TAMING THE WILDERNESS

No one knows exactly how many people were living in the Americas in the late 15th century, when the European invasion began. Historians estimate, however, that when Christopher Columbus dropped anchor in the Bahamas on his fateful voyage, there were about four million Native Americans in the region that is now the United States and Canada; today, in contrast, the population of those two countries totals about 300 million.

When the Europeans arrived, the Native Americans were spread lightly across the land. The largest communities numbered at most several thousand people—far fewer people than in London, Paris, and other fast-growing European cities of the time. Native American populations tended to remain small or to grow very slowly, which meant that they could sustain themselves without exhausting the resources of the land. In addition, most communities were nomadic, moving from place to place in accordance with the seasons, the migrations of game animals, or patterns set by religion and tradition. This nomadic way of life enabled the Native Americans to live, for the most part, in harmony with the land. When fish or game began to grow scarce, or the soil of a garden plot became less fertile, the community moved on to a new location, leaving their former home to restore itself through natural processes.

The native peoples of North America created a wide variety of cultures, but from the Inuit and Dene of the Arctic to the Hopi

Native American agriculture as depicted by German artist and publisher Theodore de Bry in 1591. The men are loosening the soil with hoes while the women plant beans and corn. When this patch of soil began to lose its fertility, the Indians would move on, letting the tilled earth return to its natural state. *(Library of Congress)*

and Zuni of the Southwest, these cultures shared one important feature: They were, as historian Richard Bartlett has said, "beautifully attuned to the environment." The Native Americans existed comfortably within the natural world; they did not see themselves as apart from the rest of nature, or set above it. The Europeans who colonized America, however, brought with them a different way of looking at the natural world. Their view of nature had been shaped over the centuries by the traditions of the Jewish and Christian religions, in which humankind is set apart from the rest of creation because only humans have souls and are created in God's image. According to Judeo-Christian tradition, humans had been created to rule the world and all living things, which exist only to serve human needs. "Be fruitful, multiply, fill the earth and conquer it," God instructs Adam and Eve in the first book of the Christian Bible. "Be masters of the fish of the sea, the birds of heaven and all living animals upon the earth." The difference between the Native American and European world views was simple but profound. Native Americans saw themselves as nature's partners. Europeans saw themselves as nature's masters.

From the very beginning, America presented more than one face to its European conquerors. On one hand, the Europeans were struck by the unspoiled loveliness of the New World. According to Bartolomé de Las Casas, a chronicler of Columbus's voyages, Columbus responded to that loveliness. After climbing a mountain in Cuba to survey the landscape, Columbus reported that "all that he had seen was so beautiful that his eyes would never tire beholding so much beauty, and the songs of the birds large and small."

On the other hand, the Europeans often viewed the new land in economic terms, wondering what they would get out of it. The day after Columbus praised the beautiful landscape, for example, he rejoiced in the wealth that Europeans could take from it. After explaining that the native inhabitants were naked and unarmed, and therefore unable to defend themselves, Columbus described the many fruits he had seen and concluded that "all should be very profitable." These two responses—admiration for natural beauty and eagerness to wrest profit from it—merged in the Europeans' vision of the Americas. To the European explorers and conquistadores, and to the monarchs and merchants who backed their ventures, the New World was a vast, fruitful, virgin paradise just waiting for them to harvest its riches and carry them home to Spain, England, or France.

In the early 17th century, as settlements took root along the eastern seaboard of North America, the colonists formed their own image of America. From the deck of the *Mayflower* in 1620, the Puritan leader William Bradford saw the American shore as "a hideous and desolate wilderness full of wilde beasts and wild men." Most settlers shared Bradford's view of America as a fearsome and dangerous wilderness. They had come from the cities of Europe, or from its villages and its tidy, long-domesticated countryside. In America, they found themselves on the very edge of an unknown continent. Before them stretched a dark forest that sheltered not only bears and wolves—predators long since driven out of the settled parts of Europe—but also natives whom most of

A 19th-century image of the Puritans settling New England. To these early settlers, clearing away the dark and threatening forest was both a vital first step toward their own survival and a God-given "errand into the wilderness." *(Library of Congress)*

the Europeans regarded as savages. The settlers felt a need to tame this wilderness, to force the chaotic natural world into their own vision of order. Some of them, particularly the Puritans of New England, felt that it was their duty to do so. In one of his sermons, a Puritan preacher named Samuel Danforth declared that God had sent the settlers on "an errand into the wilderness"—a divine mission to civilize the wild land.

The settlers rejoiced in their mission. In his 1983 book *Changes in the Land*, a study of the way human activity transformed the colonial American landscape, historian William Cronon quotes from the writings of colonist Edward Johnson, who in 1653 happily declared that "a rocky, barren bushy, wild-woody wilderness" had been changed in a single generation into "a second England." In the generations that followed, the "errand into the wilderness" became the basis of the American idea of progress. The business of changing the continent from a savage wilderness into a tame, civilized, and—above all—productive landscape would come to be viewed as the right and proper activity of the

American people. Alexis de Toqueville, a French traveler in the United States, would write in *Democracy in America* (1832):

> *In Europe, people talk a great deal about the wilds of America, but the Americans themselves never think about them; they are insensible to the wonders of inanimate nature and they may be said not to perceive the mighty forests that surround them till they fall beneath the hatchet. Their eyes are fixed upon another sight: The American people views its own march across these wilds, draining swamps, turning the course of rivers, peopling solitudes, and subduing nature.*

To the early settlers, then, America presented itself as a dark and endless forest to be hunted, cleared, plowed, and planted. Yet it would not have ocurred to them to see their actions as destructive. They saw their role as constructive and were proud of it. They were builders and makers, creating form and purpose in a landscape that was empty of everything they had known in Europe: towns, farms, churches, markets, and roads. It seemed natural to them to rebuild those familiar institutions in the new land. But only the most thoughtful or scholarly of the settlers pondered the larger meaning of their activities. Most simply struggled to survive and to make homes for their families. They had to clear spaces in the forest for their houses, which were built with the felled trees. More trees had to be cut down to clear land for gardens, pastures, and fields; these trees became fences and outbuildings. The settlers introduced pigs, sheep, cattle, and chickens. They also introduced new tools, such as guns, axes, ox-drawn plows, and horse-drawn wagons. These devices allowed a single hard-working family to cultivate more acreage and kill more game than an entire band of Native Americans. But unlike the Native Americans, who moved on when resources began to decline, the settlers from Europe built permanent homesteads and gathered in ever-growing communities.

Settlers were drawn across the sea to America by the land, which was huge, fertile, and unpeopled (except for the Native Americans, whose claims were flatly ignored by the vast majority of whites). Europe was becoming crowded—in many places, only the very wealthy could hope to acquire land. But in America, land was there for the taking, all the way to an unknown horizon. All that a settler had to do to own property was to tame it and use it.

The concept of property ownership points up another significant difference between the Europeans and the Native Americans. Among the native peoples of North America, individuals did not own land. Such a concept would have seemed ridiculous—who could *own* the earth? Communities and tribes thought of themselves as residents on the land, along with the plants and animals, and not as its owners. When different groups warred over control of a territory, they were fighting for the right to live or hunt in the region, not over an abstract concept of absolute ownership. Yet to the settlers from Europe, many of them land-starved, ownership of the land was their reward for claiming it from the wilderness and making it productive. To these Europeans, private ownership of land was the natural order of things; they burned with the desire to establish landholdings and pass them on to their children. This idea of land ownership, so foreign to the Native Americans and so fundamental to the Europeans, was the root of many misunderstandings, broken treaties, and conflicts as the whites steadily pushed the native peoples off the lands they had inhabited for centuries.

To many of the first colonists, the American wilderness was, as William Bradford claimed, "hideous and desolate." Yet another note sounds in the early accounts of the wilderness, and that note is abundance. Over and over again, explorers and settlers spoke of America as fruitful, fertile, teeming with game and fish, thick with forests of mighty timber—a cornucopia of natural riches. Along with this fruitfulness and abundance came a sense of vastness. The early settlers did not know the size or geography of the continent; they did not even know what lay a day's journey to the west. To them, as to the explorers and geographers who were trying to fill in the blanks on the map, America seemed a land of vast extent, stretching away endlessly toward the sunset.

The natural resources of such a continent, the settlers thought, must surely be inexhaustible. From the very beginning, the American colonists took pride in the immensity and richness of their land. If they cut down all the trees in one district, no matter—an endless forest loomed on the horizon. America was so big and so fertile that the settlers believed they could never run out of soil, timber, water, game and fur animals, and the other good things of the Earth. As environmental journalist and historian Philip Shabecoff has noted, "It is probably impossible to exaggerate the importance of this image of America as a land of limitless bounty in shaping the way succeeding generations of Americans thought of and used the resources of their country."

Yet in a surprisingly short time, those resources began to give out. Beaver, for example, disappeared from the waterways of eastern North America with startling suddenness. These aquatic mammals were highly valued by the Europeans, who made hats and capes from their waterproof fur. Millions of beaver pelts were shipped to London by the Hudson's Bay Company and other fur-trading firms—so many millions that the creatures had become all but extinct in eastern Canada and New England by the 1770s. To meet the insatiable demand for pelts, trappers and traders had to keep moving farther and farther west, leaving behind them rivers, lakes, and streams that had been stripped of their once-abundant beaver populations. Much of central and western North America, in fact, was first explored by the fur trappers and traders, who ranged far ahead of the settlers, having already cleared the settled regions of fur-bearing game.

The vanishing beaver is an emblem of the new economy that Europeans had brought to North America. Native Americans had shared the continent with the beaver for countless generations without affecting the beaver population. The native peoples took from the land only what they actually consumed or used. They did not accumulate large surpluses for export; resources were not drained away from the continent. Native Americans engaged in barter, but the volume of goods they traded was quite small by European standards, and resources were traded evenly—shells for skins, perhaps, or meat for dried fish. The Native Americans had developed an economy that was adapted to the land.

The Europeans, in contrast, manipulated the land to fit their economy. They introduced a market system, in which settlers not only grew food for their families but also produced tobacco and other cash crops for sale or export. Timber, game, and fish were also harvested not just for immediate use but for sale or export. In such an economy, people did not simply take what they needed to live, as in the Native American economy; they accumulated wealth in the form of valuable resources, cash, additional real estate, or manufactured goods. The market economy spread to the Native Americans, who were encouraged to trade large quantities of their resources, such as beaver pelts, for small quantities of cash or European manufactured goods, such as blankets, steel axes, guns, and liquor.

One result of the market economy was a resource drain, in which great quantities of raw materials were taken out of North America. Another result was the beginning of environmental decline, although no one in the American colonies would have used such a term. The disappearance of beaver from the East was just one warning of what was to come. But Americans were absorbed by the struggle to tame the vast new wilderness; few of them heeded such warnings.

Visitors from Europe sometimes saw matters more clearly than the colonists themselves. The Frenchman de Toqueville commented in 1832 on Americans' lack of interest in the wilderness. Decades earlier, in the mid-18th century, a Swedish naturalist named Peter Kalm had visited the American colonies. Kalm had been appalled by the colonists' wasteful exploitation of their resources. He wrote:

> In a word, the grain fields, the meadows, the forests, the cattle, etc. are treated with equal carelessness; and the characteristics of the English nation, so well skilled in these branches of husbandry, is hardly recognizable here. We can hardly be more hostile toward our woods in Sweden and Finland than they are here: their eyes are fixed on the present gain and they are blind to the future.

Bitter experience taught some colonists the need to conserve, or save and protect, their resources. As early as the 17th century, town meetings in the New England colonies had to deal with shortages of timber and firewood and with cattle pastures that were overgrazed to the point of barrenness. Community members responded to these problems by making rules to govern the cutting of timber and the grazing of cattle. These rules were the primitive ancestors of today's environmental and land-use laws.

Other environmental problems appeared early in United States history. By 1783, the year the Treaty of Paris confirmed the independence of the United States, farmers in Virginia and elsewhere were already seeking remedies for soil that had lost its fertility through overuse; among other measures, they plowed gypsum into their worn-out fields and planted clover to restore nitrogen to the topsoil. Soil had also begun to disappear through erosion. Once the thick natural mat of protective vegetation had been removed by the steel plow, rain washed the rich topsoil away at an alarming rate. President Thomas Jefferson, who took a keen interest in agriculture at his Monticello estate in Virginia, was one of many farmers who experimented with ways of controlling erosion; he found that plowing fields along the natural contours of the land, rather than in rigid patterns of straight lines, helped conserve topsoil. James Madison, who succeeded Jefferson as president, also lamented the carelessness of farmers who had exhausted the soil in regions that were once fertile. In 1818 he wrote, "With so many consumers of the fertility of the earth, and so little attention paid to the means of repairing the ravages, no one can be surprised at the impoverished face of the country."

Conserving soil and regulating the grazing of cattle were practical concerns. They had a commonsense basis in economics, for the loss of soil and the overgrazing of pastures would eventually mean dollars lost to the landowners. But a few other voices had begun to be heard in the land, and they sang the praises of the land not for its usefulness to humans but for its own sake. One colonial American who loved the wilderness was John Bartram (1699–1777), a botanist and friend of Benjamin Franklin and America's first native-born naturalist. Bartram, who lived in the Pennsylvania colony, explored the region around Lake Ontario, the Catskill Mountains of New York, and the St. Johns River district in Florida, always searching for new plant specimens. His books about his journeys sold well both in the colonies and in Europe, and they awakened in many readers an awareness of the beauty and majesty of wild America.

Another who loved the wilderness was frontiersman Daniel Boone (1734–1820). Boone is chiefly remembered as the man who opened Kentucky to white settlement; his role in frontier America was to find a route along which "civilization" could move into the wild country. Yet according to his fellow Kentuckian John

Daniel Boone led his family and the first party of settlers through the Cumberland Gap into Kentucky in 1775, beginning the great westward migration of the pioneers. American artist George Caleb Bingham, who chronicled that migration, commemorated Boone's trek in this 1851 painting. *(Library of Congress)*

Filson, who published an account of Boone's life in 1784, Boone disliked cities and settled communities, and he found his greatest pleasure in "the beauties of nature." Like the fictional character Natty Bumppo, who was created by James Fenimore Cooper in such novels as *The Deerslayer* (1841), Boone represented Americans' conflicting feelings about the untamed natural world: These woodsmen were at home in the wilderness and deeply appreciative of its glories, yet at the same time their task was to take the mystery out of the wilderness, to make the forest safe for those who came to build roads, homes, and towns. Boone and Bumppo loved the wilderness even as they lost it.

From the very beginning—from Christopher Columbus's first visit to the Caribbean—those who came from Europe to America responded with awe to the grandeur of the new land. Far stronger, however, was their need to claim that land for their own and to remake it in the image of their own cultures and traditions. Starting with the New England Puritans, American society defined itself largely through its mastery of nature, its ability to transform and exploit the wild land. But even as Americans hastened to carry out their "errand into the wilderness," a countercurrent of conservation-mindedness began to appear in American thought. Here and there, a few people questioned the errand. They mentioned the need to preserve resources or the sadness of seeing a forest fall to the ax. Some of them spoke of aesthetics, or the appreciation of beauty; they were stirred by the loveliness of unspoiled nature and regretted the disturbances brought by advancing civilization. Others were practical, concerned with protecting resources that had economic value, such as timber and soil.

Both the aesthetic and the practical approaches to conservation remained feeble in the 17th and 18th centuries, all but drowned out by the clamor of settlement and progress. Later, however, they would come together to form the origins of the American environmental movement.

CHAPTER ONE NOTES

page 2   "beautifully attuned . . ." *Richard Bartlett,* **The New Country,** p. 22.

page 2   "Be fruitful . . ." *Genesis* 1:28, **The Jerusalem Bible.**

page 3   "all that he had seen . . ." *Samuel Eliot Morison (editor and translator),* **Journals and Other Documents on the Life and Voyages of Christopher Columbus,** p. 87.

page 3   "all should be . . ." *Samuel Eliot Morison (editor and translator),* **Journals and Other Documents on the Life and Voyages of Christopher Columbus,** p. 88.

page 3   "a hideous and desolate . . ." *Leo Marx,* **The Machine in the Garden,** p. 3.

page 4   "a rocky, barren . . ." *William Cronon,* **Changes in the Land,** p. 5.

page 5   "In Europe, . . ." Quoted in *Philip Shabecoff,* **A Fierce Green Fire: The American Environmental Movement,** p. 14.

page 7   "It is probably impossible . . ." *Philip Shabecoff,* **A Fierce Green Fire: The American Environmental Movement,** p. 11.

page 8   "In a word . . ." Quoted in *Robert McHenry and Charles Van Doren (editors),* **A Documentary History of Conservation in America,** p. 172.

page 9   "With so many consumers . . ." Quoted in *Robert McHenry and Charles Van Doren (editors),* **A Documentary History of Conservation in America,** p. 276.

page 10   "the beauties of nature . . ." Quoted in *Henry Nash Smith,* **Virgin Land,** p. 62.

CHAPTER **TWO**

THE WEST AND THE CITY

Long before he became president of the United States in 1801, Thomas Jefferson gave considerable thought to the type of society that he hoped would arise in the new republic he helped create. Jefferson wanted America to be free of the social injustices of England and other European nations, which were deeply divided along class lines, with rich, aristocratic landowners at one extreme and landless, impoverished peasants at the other. In Jefferson's opinion, the ideal America would be an agricultural nation. The backbone of society would be small, independent farmers who would support themselves and their families on their own land. Jefferson's vision was of a middle ground somewhere between the raw wilderness of the American continent and the crowded, degraded conditions of Europe. He saw America as a garden, a blend of the natural and the artificial. The landscape would remain beautiful, but it would be shaped to meet human needs. Kindly tended, the Earth would supply all that its masters required.

Jefferson knew that a nation of small landowners needed one thing above all: land. He supported the federal government's decision in 1795 to sell small sections of land to the public at low prices. But he saw that the states along the East Coast were getting crowded—by 1804, the white population of the United States numbered six million. So Jefferson looked westward, to the frontier along the Ohio and Mississippi rivers and beyond the frontier to the unexplored West. The main reason he sent Meriwether

Lewis and William Clark on their historic expedition across the continent in 1804 was to scout out the possibilities for settlement in the West.

When Lewis and Clark returned from the Pacific Northwest in 1806 with glowing stories about the abundant wildlife along the Missouri River and the lush forests and fertile soil of Oregon's Willamette Valley, they launched one of the shaping movements of 19th-century America: the westward migration. Following routes pioneered by Lewis and Clark and by scores of other wilderness explorers and trappers, hundreds of thousands of settlers sought new beginnings in the wide-open West. In the 1830s and 1840s, they headed for Oregon and California along what came to be known as the Oregon Trail; then they flowed into the Southwest and the valleys of the Rocky Mountains. In the 1860s and 1870s, they homesteaded on the prairies of Kansas and Nebraska and on the high plains of the Dakotas. In some cases, settlers followed hard upon the heels of the first scouts, occupying the land before it had been mapped or thoroughly explored. Other regions were first explored by government-sponsored expeditions. The maps and reports issued by these expeditions were of great value to later settlers.

Expedition reports were widely read, and not just by people who were planning to join a wagon train for the West. The nation's eastern states were growing ever more densely populated. During the 19th century, wilderness vanished rapidly from the eastern United States, where cities, roads and railways, dams, and factories were becoming the dominant features of the landscape. Yet although the people who lived in those cities prided themselves on America's modernity and progress, they also took a passionate interest in the West, which seemed to possess the alluring grandeur and pristine wildness that had been lost in the East. Readers turned eagerly to accounts of the mysteries of the West by explorers such as John Wesley Powell and Ferdinand Vandiveer Hayden.

Powell (1834–1902) had grown up in the Ohio River Valley during the 1840s, when the controversy over slavery in the United States was rising to fever pitch. Powell's father was a preacher and abolitionist whose antislavery views made him unpopular in his community; the young John Wesley fought many fistfights with his schoolmates in defense of his father's opinions and his own. Largely self-educated, Powell developed an interest in natural history and a love of the outdoors that led him to make long journeys collecting plants and fossils—as a young man, for example, he casually walked all the way across Michigan. When the Civil War broke out, Powell volunteered at once for the Union Army, in which he rose to command his own battalion. He lost his right arm at the Battle of Shiloh but remained on active duty, winning the rank of major and the respect of generals who would be among the country's political leaders when the war ended. These powerful friends later furthered Powell's scientific career.

After the war, the plucky Powell embarked on a series of geological explorations in the West, supported at first by money from universities in his home state of Illinois and later by federal funds. He made great contributions to the scientific understanding of the West in two fields: geology and the study of Native American cultures. But it was as an adventurer, not as a scientist, that Powell captured the public imagination. Never for a moment letting his disability stand in his way, Powell boldly climbed several of the highest peaks in Colorado and Utah.

Powell's most remarkable adventure came in 1869, when he led the first expedition ever to travel by boat along the Green and Colorado rivers, including the full length of the Grand Canyon. Overcoming food shortages, savage river rapids, and the mutinous grumbling of his men, the genial Powell brought his team through the thousand-mile trip by a combination of leadership and luck. Two years later, to gather more scientific data about the canyon, Powell made the voyage again. The published account of these trips revealed for the first time the full majesty of the Grand Canyon and excited people's interest in the natural wonders of the West.

In terms of his attitude toward the resources of the West, John Wesley Powell was a man ahead of his time—"a pioneer of scientific, rational land use," as environmental historian Philip Shabecoff has described him. In 1878, while real estate speculators and land-hungry settlers were hurrying west, grabbing up as much acreage as they could possibly claim, Powell published Report on the Lands of the Arid Region, in which he warned that the region between the Great Plains and the Sierra Nevada was too

Pipe in hand, John Wesley Powell confers with Tau-gu, a chief of the Paiute people. Powell, who insisted in vain that scientific planning should precede settlement in the West, spent several months with Tau-gu's people in 1872, studying the way of life that let them survive in the arid region around the Grand Canyon. *(National Archives 57-PE-50)*

dry to support farming and cattle-raising as practiced in the East and the Mississippi River Valley. He recommended that farms and ranches in the West be planned with an eye toward prudent use of the existing water supply, and he tried to postpone the sale of public land to ill-informed settlers until after water sources had been surveyed. But people did not want to hear the truth: that most of the the West is semidesert, and that only one-fifth of the land is well watered. They wanted to believe that the West was a fertile garden, waiting for them to make it blossom, and they were in a tearing hurry to settle it. Powell's advice was ignored by the federal agencies in charge of handing out land allotments. Only after Powell's death—and several punishing droughts—did the government step in, creating the tangle of bureaucracies that have tried to regulate water rights in the West throughout the 20th century.

One of Powell's rivals for federal funding was Ferdinand Vandiveer Hayden (1829–1887), an ambitious self-promoter and a skilled, although somewhat slapdash, geologist. Hayden grew up on an uncle's farm in upstate New York. In 1845, at the age of 16, he set off on his own to seek his fortune. Hayden acquired an education by working his way through Oberlin College in Ohio, and then he qualified as a physician. His true interest lay in geology and natural history, though, and he was well launched on a career as a fossil hunter and explorer in the Dakota Territory when the Civil War broke out. After serving as a doctor with the Union forces, Hayden looked around for someone to pay him to return to the West. He found a sponsor in the Smithsonian Institution, which sent him to make a geological survey of Nebraska; his later surveys would be funded directly by the federal government.

Beginning in 1866, Hayden spent more than a decade leading teams of explorers, geologists, and mapmakers into the western territories, first to Nebraska and then farther west into the Rocky Mountains. He was told to report on the resources and economic possibilities of the lands he surveyed, and he carried out this mission with enthusiasm, providing detailed information about timber stands, veins of coal and useful minerals, farm and pasture lands, game, and even scenery that might attract visitors. Unlike most government documents, Hayden's reports were best-sellers, snatched up by developers and corporations; Hayden was "the businessmen's explorer," says William H. Goetzmann, a leading historian of western exploration. He promoted the vision of the West as a realm of endless economic opportunity.

But Hayden was also responsible for another vision of the West that arose toward the end of the 19th century: "the Tourist's West," historian Goetzmann has called it. On several of his surveys, Hayden was accompanied by William H. Jackson, America's most important frontier photographer, and Thomas Moran, a leading landscape painter. In 1871, Jackson took the first photographs ever made of the geological wonderland called Yellowstone, with its geysers, pools, and waterfalls. Moran painted huge, sweeping canvases that conveyed the immensity and brooding beauty of the western wilderness. These images immediately caught the public fancy and were widely reproduced. They helped make Americans aware that the landscape of the West included natural wonders that were national treasures.

The celebration of nature's wonders was part of the literary and philosophical movement known as romanticism, which flourished in Germany and England in the early 19th century. Focusing on the individual human spirit and on an idealized image of nature, romanticism rejected science, order and reason—ideas that had guided the development of modern society. In the United States, romanticism took the form of an intellectual movement called transcendentalism, whose best-known voice was the New England writer Ralph Waldo Emerson. To Emerson, nature was sacred, and the beauty of nature had the power to lead the human mind to God. Emerson and other transcendentalists believed that spiritual growth came from casting aside the artificial influences of "civilization" and opening oneself to the natural world. Said Emerson, "The first in time and the first in importance of the influences on the mind is that of Nature."

Henry David Thoreau (1817–1862), one of Emerson's pupils, put the transcendentalist ideal into practice. Thoreau was a unique figure in American intellectual history. He was a thoughtful eccentric who followed his conscience and nurtured his soul by cultivating his bond with nature. *Walden* (1854), Thoreau's humble account of his spiritual journey, is a classic of American literature; it is the story of his two years in an isolated cabin at

WALDEN;

OR,

LIFE IN THE WOODS.

By HENRY D. THOREAU,

AUTHOR OF "A WEEK ON THE CONCORD AND MERRIMACK RIVERS."

I do not propose to write an ode to dejection, but to brag as lustily as chanticleer in **the** morning, standing on his roost, if only to wake my neighbors up. — Page 92.

BOSTON:

TICKNOR AND FIELDS.

M DCCC LIV.

Said a neighbor in the Massachusetts town where Henry David Thoreau spent most of his life, "Henry talks about nature as though she'd been born and grew up in Concord." *Walden,* which describes the riches of a simple life lived close to nature, touched on many issues later raised by environmentalists. *(Library of Congress)*

Walden Pond in Massachusetts, a site owned by Emerson. Thoreau believed that communion with nature refreshed and enlarged the soul, and his writings on this theme contributed to the growing cult of "wilderness worship." His words have echoed down the years to inspire many of today's environmentalists, and one line from *Walden*—"In wilderness is the preservation of the world"—became a motto for much of the modern environmental movement.

Although Thoreau never ventured into the vast landscapes of the West, confining himself to trips into the Maine wilderness and sojourns in the cozier woods of Massachusetts, he touched on many environmental themes. He wrote about the unity of all life and explored the notion that the Earth itself is a living organism—a notion that reappeared in the 1970s in the work of British ecologist James Lovelock. He deplored the great harm to other life forms caused by human activity: "Who hears the fishes when they cry?" he lamented after dam-building on the Merrimack River, which flows through New Hampshire and Massachusetts, destroyed the shad migration. And by going to jail because he would not pay taxes that were being used to finance the United States' war with Mexico, Thoreau created a model for those who choose to obey their consciences rather than the law. His 1849 essay "Civil Disobedience" remains an inspiration to those modern environmentalists who take part in logging blockades and other nonviolent protests.

Thoreau was a critic of rampant "progress," and he grieved for the passing of the wilderness. He felt the sublimity of the natural world, but he also saw its fragility and the ease with which forests, rivers, and ponds could be sullied or destroyed by careless humans. He feared that the years to come would bring bigger cities, more factories, more soot and noise and waste to hide the face of nature. Thoreau died in 1862, but he rightly foresaw that the America of the late 19th and 20th centuries would be molded by industrialization and urbanization—the twin growth of manufacturing and the cities.

In the United States as well as in Great Britain, the 19th century was the age of iron and steel. Inventions such as the steam engine, the locomotive, the cotton gin, the mechanical grain thresher, and the sewing machine changed the way people lived and worked.

America's "captains of industry"—or "robber barons," in the view of those critical of their actions—built great fortunes by acquiring control of timber, coal, oil, and other resources and by operating the blast furnaces, smelters and factories that made the new mass-produced machinery of the industrial age. In his 1964 book *The Machine in the Garden,* historian Leo Marx pictured the Industrial Revolution as a clanking, smoke-belching machine advancing into the gardenlike landscape of agricultural America.

Jefferson's vision of America as a land of independent farmers on private smallholdings was swept away by the Industrial Revolution. In the middle of the 19th century, about three-fourths of all Americans still lived in the country, but the balance was already shifting toward the cities. Chicago, New York, Boston, Philadelphia, and San Francisco grew faster than ever in the final decades of the 19th century, their populations swollen by immigrants and by the flood of people leaving rural areas to seek jobs and excitement in the cities. The trend toward urbanization has continued. By 1990, fewer than one-fifth of Americans lived in the country. The rest lived in cities or in the cities' close kin, the suburbs.

Industry, technology, and urban growth brought enormous and undeniable benefits. The train and the telegraph, and later the telephone, the automobile, and the computer, made it possible for ordinary people to travel and communicate in ways that the emperors of old could not have imagined. Advances in medicine and agriculture saved lives; advances in manufacturing created jobs. Cloth and other factory-made goods were sold in vast quantities around the world, boosting America's economy. Large cities served as centers of education, the arts, and commerce; they also provided havens for immigrants from other shores. But such progress did not come without a price.

Part of the price for progress was damage to the environment—and, eventually, to the quality of human life. In Michigan and Minnesota, and then throughout the West, the timber and mining industries stripped whole regions of their trees and shoveled mountains aside to get at the riches beneath. Gold- and silver-mining operations in Nevada and elsewhere left ravaged, poisoned landscapes in their wake. Soil eroded from slopes that had been deforested. Rivers began to be polluted with sediment, sewage from the cities, arsenic and other chemicals used in mining, and waste from factories. Smoke from coal- and oil-fired burners began to hang in the air over manufacturing centers; by the end of the 19th century, cities such as Pittsburgh were wrapped in a black, lung-destroying haze.

Insults to the environment multiplied throughout the 19th century. At the same time, a few farsighted individuals began calling attention to the damage that humans were doing to the natural world. The most important of these people was a versatile Vermonter named George Perkins Marsh (1801–1882). Born as the 19th century was dawning, Marsh was an earnest and energetic soul who combined the best qualities of the practical man of business and the scholarly man of learning. He was a lawyer, teacher, and naturalist who experimented with many careers: running a sheep farm and a marble quarry, dealing in real estate, editing a newspaper, and serving in the U.S. Congress. He ended his career as the U.S. ambassador to Turkey and later to Italy. Always curious and eager to learn, Marsh mastered twenty foreign languages so that he could read works written in those languages. He also traveled as widely as his diplomatic duties allowed.

Marsh's lifelong love of the natural world led him to make careful observations of the state of nature everywhere he went, and what he saw disturbed him. As a young man he had seen soil erosion and forest loss in his native Vermont. As a world traveler he learned that throughout Europe and the Near East, human activities such as forest clearing, overgrazing, and damming of streams had harmed the land. Areas that had been lush and fertile just a few centuries earlier were now barren. Deforestation had caused rainfall to decrease and temperatures to rise. The extermination of some species of birds, animals, and insects had allowed others to flourish to the point of destructiveness—by killing birds, for example, farmers had unwittingly allowed insect pests to multiply.

In 1864, Marsh published *Man and Nature; or, Physical Geography as Modified by Human Action,* a book that reflected years of observation and study. The book was a history of people's relationship with the land in Asia, Europe, and North America. Marsh's conclusion was that human activity, intensified by tools

After trying his hand at law, business, politics, and diplomacy, George Perkins Marsh wrote *Man and Nature,* the first serious scientific study of environmental ills by an American. *(Library of Congress)*

and technology, was damaging much of the Earth. People were carelessly or ignorantly disturbing the delicate balance of nature. Humankind, said Marsh, was "everywhere a disturbing agent. Wherever he plants his foot, the harmonies of nature are turned to discord."

Marsh is important in the history of environmental thought because he was the first to say that the human impact on the natural world cannot be dismissed or ignored. Human interference with the workings of nature, he claimed, has serious, long-lasting consequences. Marsh even speculated that damage to the environment, caused by human activity, had contributed to the downfall of some of the bygone Mediterranean civilizations—a speculation with which many later historians have agreed. But Marsh did not give in to despair. He believed that with study and care, people could improve their relationship with nature, perhaps even restore some of what had been damaged. He stressed, however, that awareness and action could not wait indefinitely.

Many environmentalists today regard Marsh as the founder of their movement and *Man and Nature* as one of its basic texts. Marsh influenced John Muir, Gifford Pinchot, and other leading conservationists of the 1890s and the early 20th century. Yet in Marsh's own time, *Man and Nature* was more widely read in Europe than in the United States. In the bumptious, self-confident era after the Civil War, Americans were intoxicated by economic growth, western expansion, and the belief that they were fulfilling their destiny by completing the conquest of the continent. Most of them had no desire to worry about what they might be doing wrong. All the same, an environmental movement was beginning to take shape. Its first challenge would be to save the vanishing wilderness.

CHAPTER TWO NOTES

page 15   "a pioneer . . ." *Philip Shabecoff,* **A Fierce Green Fire: The American Environmental Movement,** p. 62.

page 18   "the businessmen's explorer . . ." *William H. Goetzmann,* **Exploration and Empire: The Explorer and the Scientist in the Winning of the American West,** p. 498.

page 18   "the Tourist's West . . ." *William H. Goetzmann,* **New Lands, New Men: America and the Second Great Age of Discovery,** p. 411.

page 18   "The first in time . . ." *Ralph Waldo Emerson,* **The American Scholar,** p. 7.

page 20   "Who hears the fishes . . ." *Henry David Thoreau,* **A Week on the Concord and Merrimack Rivers.** Quoted in *Robert McHenry and Charles Van Doren (editors),* **A Documentary History of Conservation in America,** p. 178.

page 23   "everywhere a disturbing agent . . ." *George Perkins Marsh,* **Man and Nature,** p. 36.

CHAPTER Three

THE
PRESERVATIONISTS

Over the years, the environmental movement has embraced many causes. The first of those causes, the one around which the movement took shape in the late 19th century, was the saving of the wilderness. The people who rallied to this cause were not called environmentalists—a term that had not yet come into use. They were called preservationists, or, somewhat later, conservationists, and they were a small but passionate band dedicated to keeping a significant part of America forever wild.

The wilderness preservation movement emerged during a time of change in the United States. The settling of the West was nearly complete. Industry was transforming the American landscape and the economy. The cities were growing; soon more Americans would be urban than rural. And a momentous milestone was reached when the frontier disappeared. Ever since the first colonists had hacked their homesteads out of the forests of the eastern seaboard, Americans had thought of themselves as pioneers in a frontier land. After the wilderness was driven back from New England, the Ohio Valley became the frontier; after the taming of the Ohio Valley, the frontier lay across the Mississippi. This ever-receding, ever-beckoning frontier shaped the American character, argued historian Frederick Jackson Turner in 1893. According to Turner, the experience of taming the frontier had made Americans ruggedly individualistic, democratic, and independent. But by the time Turner presented his idea, the frontier was a thing of the past. In 1890, the U.S. Bureau of the Census had announced that the "frontier," the place where settled land met unknown and unpopulated wilderness, no longer existed. No longer was there a "great unknown" waiting beyond the horizon. America had officially been tamed.

Not everyone rejoiced at the passing of the frontier. Those who shared Thoreau's love of the wilderness dreaded the very real possibility that even the most remote and magnificent landscapes would fall to the onrushing forces of civilization in the form of miners, loggers, settlers, ranchers, and land developers. These preservationists longed to preserve part of the natural landscape, so they introduced the idea of saving the land into American public life. They argued that the government should set aside some portions of the wilderness, keeping them free of private ownership and commercial exploitation. In this way both the beauty and the economic resources of the land would be preserved for future generations.

One of the first active preservationists was Frederick Law Olmsted (1822–1903), a landscape architect from Hartford, Connecticut. Olmsted believed that people's lives were enriched by contact with nature; even in the heart of the cities, he thought, there should be green spaces. He is best remembered today for designing and creating some of America's biggest urban parks— especially for Central Park in New York City, of which he was the first superintendent. But Olmsted also played a crucial role in wilderness preservation by convincing several states to set aside certain areas as protected public lands. He surveyed the Yosemite Valley for the state of California and, struck by the magnificence of Yosemite's splendid mountain landscape of granite cliffs and domes and gushing waterfalls, he urged California to set the valley aside as a state park. In 1864, the U.S. Congress turned over the valley to California, which agreed to hold Yosemite for "public use, resort, and recreation." Another of Olmsted's victories was the establishment of Niagara Falls as a public park in New York State.

Yosemite started as a state park, but America's national park system was born a few years later, after William H. Jackson's

The Great Falls of the Yellowstone in 1907. Yellowstone, America's first national park, was created in 1872 to encourage western tourism. Ever since, the park system has struggled for a balance between promoting tourism and preserving wilderness. (*Library of Congress*)

photographs alerted the nation to the wonders of Yellowstone. In 1872, recognizing the rising public interest in America's natural wonders, Congress set aside two million acres in the Wyoming and Montana territories as "a pleasuring ground for the people." This was Yellowstone National Park, the first national wilderness park in the world. In forming the park, Congress was influenced by the railroad companies, which had realized that extraordinary landscapes were a valuable commercial resource: Scenery would draw tourists, and tourists would buy train tickets. Yet although

Yellowstone was created in large part for commercial reasons, conservation also played a role. There was a growing sense that the grandest features of the national landscape—many of which were on land still owned by the federal government, especially in the West—should be both protected from development and made available to the public.

In the years that followed, other national parks were created: Sequoia, in California, in 1890; Mt. Rainier, in Washington, in 1899; Crater Lake, in Oregon, in 1902; Grand Canyon National Monument, in Arizona, in 1908; and many more. Yosemite National Park, which surrounded the state park in Yosemite Valley, was established in 1890; later, the state park was merged into the national park. The National Park Service was created in 1916 to administer the country's growing network of parks and monuments (a national monument is similar to a national park, but monuments are less tightly protected from development and commercial use).

Although America's national parks were created by acts of the federal government, the government was nudged toward its decisions by the pleas of the preservationists, who had begun to join together in groups to make their voices heard more clearly. The first group to call for wilderness preservation was the Sierra Club, founded in 1892. Its guiding spirit was John Muir (1838–1914), one of the most significant figures in American environmental history and one whose influence remains powerful today.

John Muir was born in Dunbar, Scotland. As a child, he taught himself to climb by scaling the rock walls of a nearby 15th-century castle. When he was 11, his family moved to a farm in Wisconsin. In his autobiography, *The Story of My Boyhood and Youth*, Muir described his grim life on the farm. His father made him work long hours and was so contemptuous of learning that young John had to get up at one in the morning to educate himself by reading in secret. Muir studied at the University of Wisconsin for several years but did not graduate; instead, he fled to Canada to avoid fighting in the Civil War.

Muir had always enjoyed rambling alone among forests and hills. After the war, he decided to walk to South America by "the wildest, leafiest, and least trodden way I could find." Muir's view of life was expansive and global: Instead of labeling his notebook

John Muir loved nothing better than turning his back on stressful civilization and heading into the hills. He wrote in *Our National Parks* that "wilderness is a necessity" and that "going to the mountains is going home." *(Library of Congress)*

with a mundane mailing address, he scrawled across it "John Muir, Earth-planet, Universe." On his way to South America, Muir took a detour to explore California's Sierra Nevada. Stunned by the beauty of the Yosemite Valley, he stayed there for six years, sleeping outdoors for as much of the year as possible and working as a shepherd to pay for his extremely simple way of life. He studied the natural history of Yosemite, particularly its geology, and in 1871 newspapers and magazines began publishing his articles on the valley. Some of these articles were scientific—for example, he argued that the valley had been formed over a long period of time by glaciers. Other articles were essays celebrating nature's beauty.

The eccentric shepherd-naturalist of Yosemite became famous. Writers, philosophers and students came to him for guided tours of Yosemite. Even after he left the valley to travel in Alaska, to marry, and to work on his wife's family's farm near Oakland, Muir was regarded as the voice of Yosemite. The increasing number of Americans who shared Muir's views about the sacred loveliness of the wild land wanted him for their spokesman. Muir returned to public life in the 1880s to argue for wilderness preservation—especially for increased protection for the Sierra Nevada around Yosemite Valley. For the rest of his life, he campaigned tirelessly and passionately in this cause. Spry and tough, gaunt and weathered from spending many years climbing and hiking, with bright eyes, a long white beard, and a lilting Scottish accent, Muir seemed to be the very spirit of the wilderness. If nature worship was a cult, as some claimed, then Muir was its high priest. Yet although Muir felt a reverent respect for nature as an expression of God's creative power, he also had a keen scientific understanding of how the natural world works.

Muir's long and observant intimacy with nature had taught him the basic truth at the core of the modern science of ecology: All living things are related—they are connected with each other and with the land. As Muir said, in his typically down-to-earth way, "When we try to pick out anything by itself, we find it hitched to everything else in the universe." To Muir, the contemplation of nature brought humility and an awareness that humankind is only one small part of the vast living world. Nature exists for its own sake, he believed, and not simply for the convenience of humans, who should protect and respect the natural world. Muir's deep and certain sense of the unity of all nature shines through a passage from *Travels in Alaska*:

> When we contemplate the whole globe as one great dewdrop, striped and dotted with continents and islands, flying through space with other stars all singing and shining as one, the whole universe appears as an infinite storm of beauty.

Muir's writings did more than celebrate the glories of nature. They also denounced the spoilage, waste, and greed that were already threatening forests and publicly owned resources. In *Our National Parks*, published in 1901, Muir wrote a warning about the fate of the forests that today's environmentalists are echoing a century later:

> All sorts of costly remedies have been tried and found wanting, and the costly lessons of our own experience, as well as that of every civilized nation, show conclusively that the fate of the remnant of our forests is in the hands of the federal government, and if the remnant is to be saved at all, it must be saved quickly.

Muir and other lovers of the mountains knew that threats to the wilderness would increase in the years to come. In 1892 they founded the Sierra Club to introduce people to the wilderness through nature hikes and camping trips, to educate them about the need for conservation, and to protect wilderness areas in the Sierra Nevada. Muir was the club's first president.

Although the Sierra Club concentrated on preserving the land, particularly in California, other Americans were equally concerned with saving the nation's wildlife. George Bird Grinnell (1849–1938) was a pioneer of wildlife conservation. In 1857, when Grinnell was a child, his family moved into a house on a New York City estate that had been owned by John James Audubon, an artist famous for his detailed paintings of American birds and wildlife. Fascinated by the legacy of Audubon, who had died in 1851, Grinnell became a naturalist and sportsman. He bought *Forest and Stream* magazine, a publication for hunters and lovers of the outdoors, and in its pages he wrote of the crisis facing American

Although John James Audubon, painter of American birds, died before the environmental movement got organized, he was honored by the protectors of wildlife who founded the Audubon Society. (*Library of Congress*)

wildlife. The bison that had onced roamed the plains in huge herds were almost extinct. Many species of birds were threatened, too— killed by the millions for sport or for feathers that were used to decorate women's hats and dresses.

In 1886, Grinnell invited the public to join him in a society to protect the nation's bird life. He called it the Audubon Society. More than 30,000 people answered Grinnell's call, but *Forest and Stream* did not have enough money to keep the organization going, and it soon dissolved. The following year, Grinnell and some of his prosperous friends formed a smaller, private organization called the Boone and Crockett Club. Named for pioneer frontiersmen Daniel Boone and Davy Crockett, the club was dedicated to preserving game animals and birds, primarily so that its sporting members would continue to have creatures to hunt.

The members of the Boone and Crockett Club were typical of the first generation of American conservationists. They were wealthy men from prominent families. They were well-educated—many of them had studied science or natural history—and they had enough leisure to enjoy hunting, mountaineering, and other outdoor activities. Neither Thoreau nor Muir was wealthy, but most of their early followers were both rich and socially prominent. Critics of the conservation movement claimed that the conservationists only wanted to preserve the wilderness as a private playground for the elite few who were rich enough to enjoy it. Certainly there was some truth in this claim. In its first decades, the movement was elitist, made of up wealthy white men who were amateur naturalists and sportsmen—although many of them were also true believers in the value of protecting and understanding the natural world. The accusation of elitism has lingered around the environmental movement, however, ever since its early days as the province of the privileged. The movement did not attract working-class people, people of color, and significant numbers of women until the middle of the 20th century.

Even in the early days, though, some women did play important roles in conservation. One of these women was Mrs. Augustus Hemenway, a Boston society matron who had joined Grinnell's short-lived Audubon Society. She formed a local Audubon Society in Boston in the 1890s. The publicity her group received when she urged women to stop buying hats and dresses decorated with the feathers of slaughtered birds inspired other women and men to form dozens of similar groups around the county. In 1905, the local and state Audubon groups formed the

National Audubon Society to work nationwide for the protection of birds and other wildlife. Pressure from the society led to the passage of new laws banning the sale of bird plumes and regulating bird hunting. The Audubon Society also made education a priority, founding Junior Audubon Clubs for young people and opening summer conservation camps for teachers. The Audubon Society is still a leader in environmental education; it develops programs that are used in schools and nature centers to teach people about birds, wildlife conservation, and environmental issues in general.

Birds were not the only wild creatures to get an organization of their own. People who liked to fish and who loved rivers and lakes were worrying about the nation's waterways, which were being polluted by sewage and factory wastes. In 1922, a group of sportsmen formed the Izaak Walton League to protest the damage being done to the waterways and the loss of the fish that lived in them. They took their name from Izaak Walton, a 17th-century Englishman whose book *The Compleat Angler* is a tribute to the joys of fishing and the spiritual rewards of spending time outdoors. Like the Boone and Crockett Club, the Izaak Walton League was founded because sportsmen feared that their opportunities for sport and recreation were being threatened. In 1927, the League conducted the first nationwide study of water pollution; the League also began urging legislators to enact conservation laws. The organization remains active today and is no longer focused exclusively on fishing. Although it is less well known than the Sierra Club and the Audubon Society, it contributes to efforts to protect waterways and marine life.

The founding of the Sierra Club in 1892 marked the beginning of organized environmental activity by ordinary citizens. Yet the power to protect the wilderness lay with the government, for only the government could say what was to be done with publicly owned land or pass wildlife conservation laws. As the leading preservationist of his day, John Muir had much contact with the officials responsible for deciding what the country would do with publicly owned wilderness lands. Two of the most important such officials in the early 20th century were President Theodore Roosevelt and Gifford Pinchot, the first national forester.

Roosevelt, who was president from 1901 to 1909, was an ardent hunter, one of the founders of the Boone and Crockett Club, and an amateur naturalist who loved the outdoors. He was the first president to make conservation a major issue of his administration. Among other things, Roosevelt created the nation's first 50 wildlife refuges, beginning with Pelican Island, Florida. He also established Grand Canyon National Monument (1908) and other national monuments; greatly increased the number of national parks; set aside 125 million acres of forested land as national forests; and spread the message of conservation to state governors and other government leaders. In May of 1903 Roosevelt came to Yosemite to visit Muir. The president was thrilled by the mountain setting and by Muir's infectious enthusiasm for the wilderness: "the grandest day of my life," he announced joyfully after a day and a night spent camping alone with Muir among the high peaks.

Theodore Roosevelt is rightly regarded as a conservationist president, one who saw the need to protect part of the American wilderness and took forceful action to do so. Yet although Roosevelt understood Muir's love of nature for its own sake, regardless of its usefulness to humans, he was even more influenced by another, more practical point of view—that of Gifford Pinchot, who believed that nature should be safeguarded and prudently managed for the greater good of humankind.

Pinchot (1865–1946) was born to a wealthy and prominent Pennsylvania family. He went to Europe to study scientific forestry, a form of forest management that was well established in Germany and other countries but new to the United States. The idea behind scientific forestry was to harvest timber resources efficiently, without exhausting the supply or permanently destroying the forest. Upon returning to the United States, Pinchot adopted the term *conservation* to describe this practical approach to resource management. The term had been used by George Perkins Marsh in *Man and Nature*, but under Pinchot it entered the public vocabulary; gradually, it began to be used to describe wilderness and wildlife preservation as well as resource management.

In 1898, Pinchot was made the head of the first federal forestry service. Eventually he brought the nation's publicly owned forests under the control of the Forest Service, which is part of the

Agriculture Department. The national parks, however, remained under the control of the Interior Department.

Like Muir, Pinchot hated to see public lands being ravaged by greedy timber barons, mining companies, and other special interests. He and Roosevelt strove to put the management of the public lands on a more democratic footing. They acknowledged that resources from public lands belong to all Americans, not merely to a fortunate few. But Pinchot differed sharply from Muir in his belief that forest and wilderness were there to be *used,* not worshiped or admired or studied. As environmental historian Philip Shabecoff points out, Pinchot "was not interested in preserving the landscape for its own sake" and "cared little for protecting wildlife and even less for providing recreational opportunities in the public lands." Although Muir and Pinchot both wanted to halt the rape of public lands by unregulated special interests, their reasons were quite different. Muir loved nature's beauty and believed in its power of spiritual enrichment; Pinchot respected nature as the source of economic benefits that should be wisely safeguarded. Roosevelt stood somewhere between these two points of view—but when he had to choose a side, he sided with Pinchot.

A crucial battle between Muir's aesthetic point of view and Pinchot's practical one was fought early in the 20th century over the beautiful Hetch Hetchy Valley in Yosemite National Park. The city of San Francisco and local business interests wanted to build a dam that would turn Hetch Hetchy into a giant reservoir to provide water and electric power for San Francisco. Pinchot supported this view, feeling that it was not unreasonable for public land to be used in a way that would bring practical benefits to so many people. Muir and other preservationists were appalled. Hetch Hetchy, they argued, was a remarkable geologic formation, as beautiful and as worthy of protection as Yosemite Valley; moreover, it was already part of a national park. Was the protection offered by the nation's park system nothing more than a sham?

Muir claimed that making Hetch Hetchy into a reservoir would be like turning a church into a big water barrel. "These temple destroyers, devotees of ravaging commercialism," he said of the dam builders in the closing lines of *The Yosemite* (1912), "seem to have a perfect contempt for Nature, and, instead of lifting their eyes to the God of the mountains, lift them to the Almighty Dollar. Dam Hetch Hetchy! As well dam for water-tanks the people's cathedrals and churches, for no holier temple has ever been consecrated by the heart of man."

The fight over Hetch Hetchy was long and bitter, but in the end, Roosevelt sided with Pinchot, and Congress approved the Hetch Hetchy dam in 1913. Muir died the following year. It is often said that he died of a broken heart over the loss of Hetch Hetchy, but this is merely a touching myth. Although Muir was deeply saddened and disappointed by the outcome of the struggle, there is no evidence that it killed him.

The fight over Hetch Hetchy Valley points to an early rift in the environmental movement. On one side were those who wanted to preserve nature in its original state. On the other side were those who wanted to conserve nature as a valuable resource and to use it efficiently. That rift has widened in the years since Hetch Hetchy. From the start it divided the Forest Service, which regards the national forests as timber farms, and the Park Service, which focuses on recreation and protection and whose second director urged park workers, "Keep large sections of primitive country free from the influence of destructive civilization." As shown in the heated disputes of the 1990s over logging in national forests and cattle-grazing on public lands, the rift between those who would preserve the wilderness and those who would profit from it has widened into a Grand Canyon of controversy.

CHAPTER THREE NOTES

page 29   "the wildest, leafiest . . ." *John Muir,* **A Thousand Mile Walk to the Gulf, in The Eight Wilderness-Discovery Books,** p. 119.

page 31   "When we try to pick out . . ." *John Muir,* **The Eight Wilderness-Discovery Books,** p. 19.

page 32   "When we contemplate . . ." *John Muir,* **Travels in Alaska,** in **The Eight Wilderness-Discovery Books,** p. 724.

page 32   "All sorts of remedies . . ." *John Muir,* **Our National Parks,** in **The Eight Wilderness-Discovery Books,** p. 604.

page 36   "the grandest day of my life . . ." Quoted in *Roderick Nash,* **Wilderness and the American Mind,** p. 138.

page 37   "was not interested . . ." *Philip Shabecoff,* **A Fierce Green Fire: The American Environmental Movement,** p. 69.

page 37   "These temple destroyers . . ." *John Muir,* **The Yosemite,** in **The Eight Wilderness-Discovery Books,** p. 716.

page 38   "Keep large sections . . ." Quoted in *Philip Shabecoff,* **A Fierce Green Fire: The American Environmental Movement,** p. 85.

CHAPTER **Four**

THE ECOLOGISTS

During the first half of the 20th century, wilderness preservation was eclipsed in American public and political life by the challenges of two world wars (1914–18 and 1939–45) and the severe economic depression of the 1930s. During the Great Depression, conservation became linked to jobs when the federal government created the Civilian Conservation Corps, which put unemployed people to work building roads in national forests and constructing dams and irrigation canals. For the most part, the public's focus on the natural world during this period was on resource development, not on preservation.

After John Muir's death, the Sierra Club largely withdrew from the preservation fight, licking the wounds it had received over Hetch Hetchy. The club continued to introduce thousands of people to nature through its hikes and ski trips, but it had become primarily a recreational organization. The Sierra Club also retained an air of elitism; people who wished to join the club had to be sponsored by two members, and many of the members came from the upper ranks of business and the professions. New groups, however, were being formed as people came together to protect the wilderness from the rising tide of technology, population growth, and economic exploitation.

One of these new groups was the National Wildlife Federation, founded by an Iowa-born political cartoonist and nature lover named J. N. Darling, known to his friends and fans as "Ding" Darling. In 1934, Darling was made head of the Biological Survey, an agency established by the federal government to supervise research on the nation's wildlife and to oversee hunting and fishing laws. A fervent believer in wildlife preservation, Darling became convinced that swift and strong federal action was needed to protect wetlands, waterways, and forests, the vital habitats of birds and other creatures. In a speech at the first North American Wildlife Conference in 1936, Darling urged nature societies and state and local wildlife associations to get involved in politics. He pointed out that there were at that time more than 35,000 clubs or organizational chapters in the United States devoted to the study of nature, the enjoyment of the wilderness, or the protection of wildlife. Yet the members of these associations had never elected a single public official—not even a local dog-catcher. Darling called for a greater sense of purpose and unity among these scattered groups and declared that the only way to achieve their goals was through political action. Conservationists, he declared, must make their voices heard through lobbying, campaigning, voting, and running for office.

People interested in conservation responded to Darling's call. They organized the General Wildlife Federation and elected him its president; the name was changed to the National Wildlife Federation (NWF) in 1938. At first, like many preservation groups, the NWF appealed mostly to hunters. Gradually, however, its membership base broadened. From the start, the NWF proved to conservationists that they could make a difference through organized political action. In 1937, the NWF helped push a law through Congress that taxed firearms and gave the money to state wildlife protection programs. The NWF also directed its energies toward educating the public. It sponsored National Wildlife Week to spread the word about the threats to America's wild birds and animals, and it launched several books and magazines for children. The most successful of these was *Ranger Rick,* a monthly magazine that used stories, pictures, and games to teach children about wildlife and about the basics of wilderness conservation— preventing forest fires, for example.

The NWF got results by using the political clout of a large, organized group. Another group, formed a few years later, used its pocketbook to get things done. In 1951, concerned scientists decided to do something about the loss of natural habitats and the resulting threat to the plants and animals that needed those habitats to survive. Instead of going through government channels, they turned to the old-fashioned American tradition of private enterprise. They founded the Nature Conservancy, a nonprofit organization that takes direct action to save key habitats, such as a New Jersey marsh that serves as a crucial resting place for millions of migratory birds, or a stretch of Florida beach where endangered sea turtles come ashore to lay their eggs. The Conservancy buys land in these places and sets it aside for preservation and study. With money raised from members and corporate donors, the Nature Conservancy has bought more than 7.5 million acres in the 50 states and Canada; in addition, the Conservancy works with conservation groups in Latin America to promote habitat preservation and wildlife study there. Today the Conservancy owns the world's largest privately owned system of nature sanctuaries: 1,300 preserves, many of them open to the public.

In the 1930s, John Muir's role of wilderness prophet and protector was taken up by a young man named Robert Marshall. Marshall is little known today to the general public, but he was immensely important to the modern environmental movement. In his short lifetime, he restored passion and spiritual meaning to the preservationist crusade.

The son of a prominent lawyer, Marshall was born in 1901 and grew up in New York City. Like many environmentalists, he enjoyed early contact with the natural world. He spent summer vacations in the Adirondack Mountains of New York State, where he became a skilled and enthusiastic mountain climber at an early age. Before he was 21, he had climbed the 46 highest peaks in the Adirondacks. Later he explored in Alaska. All his life he was an ardent hiker, routinely covering 30 or more miles a day with a bedroll and knapsack strapped to his back. Yet although Marshall loved the solitude of wild places, he was not an unsociable loner. His associates remembered him as humorous, compassionate and companionable; he was also committed to liberal values such as civil rights and equal opportunities for all people. Marshall took an interest in socialism and other economic and political concepts that had become deeply unpopular with the American business and political establishment by the late 1930s. These interests are reflected in his 1933 book *The People's Forests*, in which he argued that the public, not private individuals or companies, was the most fitting owner of forest and wilderness land, and that "social welfare [should be] substituted for private gain as the major objective for management."

Marshall studied forestry and went to work for the U.S. Forest Service. His experiences on the job made him critical of both the Forest Service and the Park Service. He felt they were more concerned with building roads, cutting timber, and opening stores and lodges to lure tourists than with preserving the wilderness in anything like its natural state. In 1930 he wrote an essay entitled "The Problem of the Wilderness" for *Scientific Monthly*. In this article, a key document in environmental history, Marshall described the kind of roadless, undisturbed wilderness areas that he thought should be preserved within America's public lands. Marshall called for a new organization made up of "spirited people who will fight for the freedom of the wilderness."

In 1935, Marshall and a handful of other "spirited people" founded the Wilderness Society to lobby for the preservation of true wilderness areas, as distinct from national parks and forests that were easily reached by road and had been developed for recreation or exploitation. Marshall was the Wilderness Society's main financial supporter until his sudden death four years later at the age of 38. The Society lost some of its drive during the 1940s, but in the 1950s, under a new director named Howard Zahniser, it resumed the crusade with letters, petitions, public education, and political maneuvering at the national level.

In 1955, Zahniser wrote and proposed to Congress an act calling for the designation of 50 million acres of public land as permanent wilderness, to be forever closed to mining, logging, and dam-building. For nearly a decade, conservationists fought to get the act passed into law. Faced with opposition from business interests and from government agencies such as the Forest Service, the backers of the act had to make many compromises. After 18 congressional hearings and 66 revisions, the Wilderness Preservation Act was finally passed in 1964. It set aside 9.1 million acres of wilderness for protection and included ways to add new wilderness areas in the future, but it also allowed some mining, grazing, dam-building, and recreational development in the wilderness areas. Zahniser died a few months before the act became law. His fellow conservationists hailed the passage of the act; they also recognized, however, that it had been weakened by the inevitable give and take of the political process. Under the act, one of the most rugged and pristine areas in the nation, located in Montana, was named the Bob Marshall Wilderness in honor of the Wilderness Society's founder.

To Marshall, as to Muir, unspoiled wilderness was the loveliest part of nature. Preserving it had the quality of a sacred or spiritual mission. The beauty of such places, Marshall believed, was best felt in solitude, by those willing to hike and climb and to sleep outdoors. Marshall realized that not everyone can or wants to become a wilderness explorer; still, he felt that *everyone* could benefit from time spent in the "green utopia" of the forest, as a retreat from the pressures of civilization and urban life. He suggested that the government should not only maintain state and national parks for the use of ordinary tourists and vacationers but should also provide transportation and camps for low-income people, so that "nature" would not belong only to those who had the money to enjoy it. Marshall's ideas about social reform, which included an undercurrent of extreme and sometimes radical change, are often overlooked by scholars who focus mainly on his love of the wilderness; but his radical ideas were also part of his legacy to the environmental movement.

Conservationism entered a new phase with Aldo Leopold, who helped Marshall found the Wilderness Society. Leopold was born in 1887 in Iowa. Like Marshall, he was trained as a forester; he worked for Gifford Pinchot in the Forest Service. Leopold started his career as a resource-oriented forester, one who thought that public lands should be made to yield the highest possible economic benefits to society. During the 1920s and 1930s, his studies of wildlife habitats in the public lands convinced him that human population growth and economic demands were placing too great a strain on the natural world, destroying parts of it forever: "Wilderness is a resource that can shrink but not grow," he sadly observed. Leopold agreed with Marshall that parts of the forest lands should be preserved without roads, trails, or buildings, and he wrote a blizzard of essays in support of the Wilderness Society's goals.

Leopold earned a place in environmental history by introducing the general public to a new way of regarding nature—the way

Aldo Leopold's *A Sand County Almanac* (1949) gave many readers their first glimpse of the natural world as a huge, interlinked community—one in which human beings had not yet recognized their true place. *(Wilderness Society)*

of the ecologist. Ecology is a fairly new science. The term *ecology* was coined by German biologist Ernst Haeckel in 1869 and refers to the study of the relationships among living things and their environment. The ecologist does not simply study fish, for example, as a traditional biologist might. The ecologist studies the fish and their ecosystem: the things they eat, the things that eat them, the river or lake in which they live, the climate and weather that affect that lake, the other creatures that live in the lake, and so on. Ecology, in other words, looks at the big picture. Thoreau and Muir, too, had talked of the interconnectedness of all life, but the ecological perspective grew out of painstaking scientific study as well as philosophical musing.

Aldo Leopold's gift to environmentalism was his ability to express ecological insights in simple, poetic language that all could understand. This gift is best revealed in *A Sand County Almanac*, a collection of Leopold's writings that was published in 1949, a year after his death. The book begins with deceptive simplicity, describing in short but moving essays the passage of the seasons on Leopold's Wisconsin farm. The theme of loss, of the irreversible destruction of prairies and rivers and forests, echoes through these essays. *A Sand County Almanac* concludes with a plea for what Leopold called "a land ethic," a new way of behaving toward the natural world. He hoped that humans would learn that the natural world is not a commodity that they possess but rather a community that they inhabit. People have developed codes of ethical behavior to govern their relationships with others in the human community; said Leopold, "The land ethic simply enlarges the boundaries of the community to include soils, waters, plants, and animals, or collectively: the land."

Leopold's insistence that people are not the conquerors of nature, but only a part of it, became a cornerstone of the modern environmental movement. His call for a new relationship between people and the land has inspired and guided many of today's environmentalists. Dave Foreman, who helped found the radical Earth First! movement in 1981, called *A Sand County Almanac* the most important book of the 20th century.

After Leopold, the wilderness preservation movement was strengthened by the ecologists' growing understanding of the natural world. The voices of hunters and nature lovers were joined by a chorus of scientists, who pointed out that humankind knew next to nothing about complex ecological interrelationships and should not be in such a hurry to destroy what was only imperfectly understood.

A Sand County Almanac was one of the first books in a wave of nature writing that combined thoughtful philosophy, high-quality prose, and the broad perspective of the knowledgeable ecologist. Some of the authors of these influential books were trained scientists; others were gifted writers who had absorbed the ecological point of view. Among them were anthropologist Loren Eiseley, who reflected on the links between humans and the rest of the natural world in *The Immense Journey* (1957) and *The Star-Thrower* (1978); naturalist Joseph Wood Krutch, who in the 1950s explored and wrote about the Baja Peninsula, the Grand Canyon, and the deserts of the Southwest; wildlife biologist Olaus Murie, whose wife and traveling companion Margaret Murie wrote about their field trips in Alaska; Marjory Stoneman Douglas, whose 1947 book *The Everglades: River of Grass* is the classic description of the Florida wetlands; and historian and conservationist Wallace Stegner, who wrote penetratingly about the ecology of the American West in such books as *Beyond the Hundredth Meridian: John Wesley Powell and the Second Opening of the West* (1954) and *Where the Bluebird Sings to the Lemonade Springs* (1992).

These and other ecologist-writers not only stimulated readers' interest in wilderness and wildlife but performed two other vital services as well. First, they established a tradition of nature writing that has become a flourishing part of American literature, producing award-winning books such as Barry Lopez's *Arctic Dreams* (1986), Bill McKibben's *The End of Nature* (1989), and Sallie Tisdale's *Stepping Westward* (1991). Second, the ecologist-writers introduced the reading public to the broad ecological view of nature. Terms drawn from ecological science, such as *environment*, *habitat*, *biodiversity*, and *ecosystem*, were brought into the American vocabulary by Leopold and those like him.

Ecology is now firmly established as an important part of the American environmental movement. This scientific strain of environmentalism has been represented in recent years by scientists who combine research, usually in some aspect of biology, with environmental activism. These scientists have included Dian

Ecologist Edward O. Wilson, one of many scientists who have taken up the cause of environmental protection, warns that the mass extinction of species today impoverishes humanity's future: "We should not knowingly allow any species or race to go extinct." *(Courtesy of Edward O. Wilson)*

Fossey, whose fierce devotion to the study and protection of African mountain gorillas cost her her life at the hands of soldiers or poachers who resented her conservation activities; oceanographer Sylvia Earle, whose studies of undersea life around the world have convinced her of the need to halt ocean pollution and reef destruction; and zoologist Edward O. Wilson, who has contributed to the scientific study of organisms ranging from ants to human beings. In his book *The Diversity of Life* (1992), Wilson surveys the current worldwide destruction of ecosystems and species and warns that "the green prehuman earth is the mystery we were chosen to solve, a guide to the birthplace of our spirit, but it is slipping away." Like other contemporary ecologists, Wilson echoes Leopold's call for action based on a better understanding of humankind's place in the world. "An enduring environmental ethic," he says, "will aim to preserve not only the health and freedom of our species, but access to the world in which the human spirit was born."

CHAPTER FOUR NOTES

page 43   "social welfare . . ." Robert Marshall. Quoted in *Robert Gottlieb,* **Forcing the Spring: The Transformation of the American Environmental Movement,** p. 17.

page 43   "spirited people . . ." *Robert Marshall,* "The Problem of the Wilderness," **Scientific Monthly,** February 1930, p. 148.

page 44   "Wilderness is a resource . . ." *Aldo Leopold,* **A Sand County Almanac,** p. 199.

page 46   "The land ethic . . ." *Aldo Leopold,* **A Sand County Almanac,** p. 204

page 46   Foreman on Leopold. In *Susan Zakin,* **Coyotes and Town Dogs: Earth First! and the Environmental Movement,** p. 28.

page 49   "the green prehuman earth . . ." *Edward O. Wilson,* **The Diversity of Life,** p. 344.

page 49   "An enduring environmental ethic . . ." *Edward O. Wilson,* **The Diversity of Life,** p. 351.

CHAPTER Five

SOUNDING THE ALARM

To many Americans, the issues of wilderness and wildlife preservation seemed rather remote. But another type of environmentalism was emerging, driven not by love of natural beauty but by fear. In the middle years of the 20th century, environmentalists such as Rachel Carson called attention to the ways in which ecological damage threatened human well-being. Their arguments were not about scenic landscapes that only a small percentage of Americans would ever see; they were about people's health, and the health of their children. Carson and others like her who sounded the alarm about environmental hazards made millions of Americans sit up and take notice. Many people who had not worried about the loss of resources or wilderness were jolted into environmental awareness by the threat to human life.

Rachel Carson (1907–1964) was born in the small town of Springdale in western Pennsylvania. Her life and work were shaped by three passions: her love of the sea, her interest in scientific research, and her delight in writing about nature. Carson became a biology teacher and then, in the 1930s, went to work as a biologist at a U.S. Fish and Wildlife Service research station in Patuxent, Maryland. Not only was she exposed to all the newest biological and oceanographic research from around the world, but she also had the opportunity to study the ocean in all seasons and all weathers. She began writing about the sea, and her break-

A contemplative researcher who rose to the challenge of tackling the powerful chemical industry, Rachel Carson showed Americans one possible future: a sick, silent world without birdsong. *(Library of Congress)*

through as an author came in 1951, when *The New Yorker* magazine published three articles that Carson later issued as a book called *The Sea Around Us.*

The book was an immediate and remarkable best-seller, as was Carson's next book, *The Edge of the Sea.* Carson was able to retire and devote herself to writing, for which she possessed a rare combination of qualities. Her style was simple and easy to read, yet she used vivid language that touched readers' emotions. Her deep understanding of science and her joy in communicating its wonders to others were blended with a passionate concern for the ocean and its life. Carson rejected the notion that science was too difficult or too complicated for the ordinary person to understand; she did not want people to think of scientists as "isolated and priestlike in their laboratories." When she accepted the National Book Award for *The Sea Around Us,* she said, "Science is part of the reality of living; it is the what, the how, and the why in everything in our experience." Her mission was to help people understand how science could explain their lives and the life around them.

Carson never married. Throughout her life she devoted much care to family members, but she was happiest on her own, living next to her beloved sea, studying and writing. Soft-spoken and shy, Carson learned to cope with the demands of fame when the success of her books shot her into public view. But the attention that came her way after *The Sea Around Us* was nothing compared with the storm stirred up by her most important book, *Silent Spring.* Carson was drawn into writing this controversial book by a friend named Olga Owens Huckins, who lived in Duxbury, Massachusetts. In 1958, Duxbury was sprayed with a powerful insecticide called DDT (dichloro-diphenyl-trichloroethane) that was widely used to kill mosquitoes. Huckins, a bird lover, was horrified when some of the birds in her yard died what she described as "agonizing deaths." She was certain that the DDT was to blame and asked Carson to investigate. Carson set aside the articles on which she was working and agreed to look into the pesticide problem. Thus began a new era in environmentalism.

By the 1950s, DDT and dozens of similar compounds were being used in the United States to kill insects and other irritating or crop-destroying pests such as slugs and rodents. These pesticides, together with chemical fertilizers and weed-killers, were key elements of the so-called "Green Revolution"—the technological wizardry that boosted crop yields around the world in the years after World War II. As symbols of the postwar success of American science and industry, chemicals were promoted through industry-produced "news" films, magazine articles praising the virtues of the chemical industry, and slogans such as "Better Living Through Chemistry." But Carson discovered that very little impartial research had been done about the long-term effects of these chemicals. To her amazement, she found that nearly all of the published studies of the most widely used compounds had been prepared by scientists who worked for the chemical industry. She set out to learn more, and she started by tracking down reports of dead fish and birds and sick farm workers who had been exposed to DDT and other chemicals. As she gathered information from biologists and field researchers, she realized that some frightening facts about pesticides were utterly unknown to the general public.

At first, Carson tried to sell an article on pesticides to magazines, but several editors turned her down because they did not want to lose the income from chemical-industry ads. Carson then turned her article into a book called *Silent Spring*. She found a publisher in the Houghton Mifflin Company of Boston, although a large chemical manufacturer called the Veliscol Corporation threatened to sue Houghton Mifflin to keep the book from appearing, claiming that Carson was irresponsibly trying to turn people against the chemical industry. Carson and her publisher stood firm, however, and Veliscol backed down. Large sections of *Silent Spring* appeared as articles in *The New Yorker* in 1962, just before the book was issued.

Carson had used of all her writer's skills and her environmentalist's passion, and *Silent Spring* made an instant and powerful impression. It opens with a charming description of a town in "the heart of America" waking to the morning chorus of birdsong. Then the birds begin to die. Cows and chickens grow ill. So do children. Some die. The "grim specter" that has crept over the town, Carson warns, "may easily become a stark reality we all shall know."

The basic message of *Silent Spring* is that synthetic pesticides such as DDT linger in animal tissue and in soil and water, poisoning not just the pests at which they are aimed but also many other creatures and, ultimately, the environment itself. The poisons interfere with the ability of birds to reproduce; they also travel up through the food chain until, in the flesh of birds, fish, and larger animals, they are consumed by humans. People can suffer immediate and severe illnesses from chemical poisoning. In addition, future effects are impossible to predict and may include birth defects and genetic damage. Carson claimed that the whole world was being used as a gigantic laboratory experiment, without the informed consent of the lab's human population. "For the first time in the history of the world," she wrote, "every human being is now subjected to contact with dangerous chemicals from the moment of conception until death."

Carson's purpose was not merely to inform people; she hoped also to frighten them and thus rouse them to action. She wanted citizens to understand the ecological principle of interconnectedness and to insist on government regulations shaped by partnership with nature, not dominance of it. Like many of today's environmentalists, she urged farmers and the agribusiness industry to use alternatives to synthetic pesticides—for example, allowing beneficial insects and birds to prey on pest populations.

The publication of *Silent Spring* made Rachel Carson the center of a heated debate that continued long after her death from cancer 18 months later. The book won her many supporters, but it also made enemies. The most vicious offensive came from the chemical industry, which answered *Silent Spring* with a salvo of advertisements, book reviews, and articles written by pesticide experts from within the industry. Not content with questioning Carson's facts and ideas, some critics descended to the level of personal attack, suggesting that as a woman Carson was bound to be a second-rate scientist, incapable of understanding complex chemical reactions. A few went so far as to hint that she was a communist or a lesbian—two labels that were equally unacceptable in early 1960s America. Carson was also labeled a crank and an alarmist. The former science editor of *Newsweek* magazine accused her of trying "to scare the American public out of its wits"—and, in a sense, he was right, although his comment was meant as an insult.

But a large portion of the American public responded with interest and concern to Carson's message. People began asking questions about pesticide residues and public health, about corporations' right to make money regardless of the consequences, and about federal regulation of the chemical industry. Carson's work produced results. Largely as a result of the public feeling stirred up by *Silent Spring*, DDT was banned in the United States in 1971 (although U.S. corporations continue to make and sell it in other countries). Carson's legacy also includes the many people who first identified themselves as environmentalists as a result of reading her works. She built bridges to connect ecology, wildlife protection, public health, and political activism; hundreds of people entered the environmental movement over those bridges.

Rachel Carson had sounded the alarm about chemical threats to environmental and human health. Other alarm bells were warning the public of other dangers. An incident in Los Angeles in 1943, in which deaths and illnesses were caused by high concentrations of smoke, dust, and soot in the air, had alerted the U.S. public to a new menace: smog. Donora, a steel town in Pennsylvania, suffered an even worse episode of air pollution in 1948. Soon "smog" and "air pollution" were entering the everyday conversation of people across the country. "Water pollution" became a household term, too, when the foam from synthetic laundry detergents was identified as a leading culprit in the spoilage of the nation's waterways. And by the 1960s, concern about litter and garbage along roads and highways had become a topic of national discussion. These issues added more facets to the environmental movement as people began to examine the root causes of litter and pollution. Ecologists and conservationists grew increasingly critical of America's dependence on cars, consumption, and sky-darkening fossil fuels.

As though pesticide residues and pollution were not enough "to scare the American public out of its wits," the prospect of nuclear annihilation or radioactive contamination terrified quite a few people, including some of the scientists who had developed atomic technology in the first place. In the years after World War II, scientists and citizens formed a number of organizations to educate the public about the dangers of nuclear technology, in bombs or in power plants. Among these antinuclear groups were the Federation of Atomic Scientists, founded in Chicago in 1945 by scientists who had worked on the top-secret Manhattan Project to make the first atomic bombs; a national association of citizens' committees called SANE, founded in 1957, which organized large antinuclear demonstrations in the late 1950s and the 1960s; scores of student groups that opposed nuclear technology as part of the antiwar movement of the late 1960s and the early 1970s; the Union of Concerned Scientists, founded at the Massachusetts Institute of Technology in 1969; and many local and regional groups organized to shut down nuclear power plants or prevent them from being built in the first place. These groups made the antinuclear movement a flourishing wing of the larger environmental movement.

A handful of environmentalists focused on population growth and its threat to the world's resources and to the quality of life. One of the first American thinkers to tackle the population problem was Fairfield Osborn, a conservationist and president of the New York Zoological Society who carried on a family tradition of interest in nature: His father had been a biologist and president of the American Museum of Natural History in New York City. Osborn's book *Our Plundered Planet* (1948) reintroduced the ideas of Thomas Malthus, an English economist and historian who had demonstrated in 1798 that populations grow faster than their food supply can increase. Malthus had warned that human population growth would eventually outstrip people's ability to feed themselves, with mass starvation and suffering as the outcome.

Where Malthus had considered countries or regions, Osborn applied Malthusian thinking to the entire world and concluded that the skyrocketing global population, growing faster than ever after World War II, was headed for a food crisis. Osborn feared that world leaders, dazzled by new advances in medicine, chemistry, and agriculture, would fall into the trap of thinking that technology could bail humankind out of every crisis. "The miraculous succession of modern inventions," he wrote, "has so profoundly affected our thinking as well as our everyday life that it is difficult for us to conceive that the ingenuity of man will not be able to solve the final riddle—that of gaining subsistence from the earth." He added a somber warning against placing too much faith in science's synthetic creations: "The grand and ultimate illusion would be that man could provide a substitute for the elemental workings of nature." Osborn created the Conservation Foundation to sponsor and publish research on overpopulation and resource management.

Our Plundered Planet sparked many debates about population, resources, and technology during the 1950s. On one side were those who argued, like Thomas Nolan, director of the U.S. Geological Survey, that the "inexhaustible resource of technology" could solve any problems the future might bring. On the other side were those who agreed with Osborn that the combination of an ever-growing world population and ever-shrinking resources (disappearing forests, topsoil and petroleum deposits) was likely to cause trouble that technology might not be able to remedy.

The debate over population growth and its role in environmental and public-health problems continues today. Some observers claim that although population is growing at an unprecedented rate, such growth is a good thing. Economist Julian Simon, for example, argued in *The Ultimate Resource* (1981) that population growth is necessary for economic growth, and that more people will simply mean more minds to invent solutions to the resource shortages of the future. The opposing point of view is best represented by biologist Paul Ehrlich, whose 1968 book *The Population Bomb* described the overcrowded world of the future and predicted global environmental and public-health breakdowns as a result of runaway population growth. The book became a surprise best-seller, catapulting the population issue out of the universities and research institutes and into the mass media and public discussion.

Ehrlich had touched a sensitive nerve, and many Americans apparently agreed that overpopulation was a worrisome issue. After *The Population Bomb* appeared, Ehrlich helped found an organization called Zero Population Growth (ZPG), and by 1970 ZPG had more than 33,000 members in 380 chapters across the United States. ZPG's goals were to make population growth an issue for government and environmentalists, to provide information about the issue, and to encourage people to limit family size to two children per family. ZPG remains a leader in research and education about population growth and its connections to poverty, public health, and the environment. ZPG also urges support for programs that give people control over family size—for example, clinics that offer voluntary sterilizations or birth-control supplies.

The energetic and articulate Ehrlich has become a frequent speaker at conferences and campuses around the world; he has also continued to explore the relationships among population, health, and environmental ills in a stream of publications, many written with biologist Anne Ehrlich, his wife. In 1990 the Ehrlichs published *The Population Explosion,* in which they reviewed the consequences of the jump in world population from 3.5 billion in 1968 to 5.3 billion in 1990 and concluded, "The greatest need today is for better understanding of the urgency of population reduction, as well as for reducing individual impacts on our battered planet." Even within the environmental movement, however, some people find the idea of controlling population growth disagreeable. Critics of population control have linked the discussion of overpopulation with such potentially explosive subjects as abortion, religious and personal freedom, and differences in family size among racial and ethnic groups and economic classes. Partly because of its links with these volatile subjects, overpopulation is perhaps the most complex issue facing the environmental movement today, although some environmentalists, like most world leaders, prefer to avoid discussing it.

A few influential thinkers of the 1960s and 1970s blamed environmental problems not on the growing population but on destructive technology, the careless and wasteful habits of businesses and consumers, and, underlying everything, the basic structure of society and the economy. In his 1962 book *Our Synthetic Environment,* ecologist Murray Bookchin criticized urban sprawl and society's increasing dependence on large-scale industry, especially the chemical and nuclear industries. Bookchin insisted that the natural environment could not be healthy unless the social order was ecologically healthy. He called for a radical reorganization of society into small, decentralized regions, in which technology would be based on ecologically sound principles, such as replacing combustible fossil fuels with solar and wind power, and in which the economy would be tailored to the regional environment and to people's actual needs, not to corporations' need to make money. Although Bookchin's ideas are too extreme for most mainstream environmentalists, they have attracted some earnest followers who claim that environmental salvation demands a basic restructuring of society.

Like Bookchin, Barry Commoner has proposed radical solutions to environmental problems. Born in Brooklyn in 1917, Commoner became a biologist. In the 1950s, while teaching at Washington University in St. Louis, Missouri, he organized a committee of scientists to protest the above-ground testing of nuclear weapons. The committee studied the levels of radioactive elements in babies' teeth and proved that testing was spreading radioactive fallout, creating a serious public-health risk. Thanks largely to the vigorous efforts of Commoner and other scientists, including Nobel Prize–winner Linus Pauling, the United States, the Soviet Union, and a hundred other nations agreed in 1963 to stop testing nuclear devices in the Earth's atmosphere and in the sea. France and China refused to sign the test-ban treaty, however, and carried out nuclear tests in the atmosphere and underwater after 1963; other nations, including the United States, have continued to test nuclear devices underground.

Commoner remained involved with the antinuclear movement but broadened his concerns to cover the range of environmental ills that emerged in the 1950s, 1960s, and 1970s. He argued that "the enveloping cloud of science and technology" was destroying the natural world with toxic pollution. In Commoner's best-known book, *The Closing Circle* (1972), he claimed that setting "acceptable limits" on pollution did not go far enough. Pollution should be banned entirely; new, ecologically safe technologies should be devised to replace the destructive technology of the present day. Decisions about resources, technology, and the environment should be made by an informed and empowered public and based on sound science, not on the interests of big corporations or bloated government bureaucracies. Most provocatively, Commoner declared that socialism—the ownership of resources and factories by the public rather than by private individuals or corporations—was the way to save the environment.

Commoner's talk of socialism alarmed many people within the environmental movement, who feared that attacks on the capitalist economic system or on the prevailing social order would alienate Americans who might otherwise support wilderness preservation or pollution control. Yet Commoner has attracted a substantial following among students, intellectuals, and activists who agree with him that trying to fix each separate environmental problem without changing the social and economic systems that have let those problems arise is like putting a Band-Aid on a patient who is bleeding to death: too little, too late.

With his keen scientific understanding, his peppery wit, and his uncompromising opinions, Commoner has been both an inspiration and an irritant to other environmentalists, who have not escaped his scathing criticisms. In the late 1960s and the 1970s he was one of America's best-known scientists; on February 2, 1970, he appeared on the cover of *Time* magazine with a headline that read "Ecologist Barry Commoner: The Emerging Science of Survival." Bespectacled, crowned with a thatch of bristly white hair, and often seen in shirtsleeves without the encumbrance of a necktie, Commoner appeared frequently in the news. He not only made his views clear in scores of books, articles, and speeches but also took them into the political arena. In 1979 he made an unsuccessful run for president as the Citizens Party candidate; in 1984 he became an environmental advisor to Democratic presidential hopeful Jesse Jackson.

Throughout the 1950s and 1960s, the environmental movement took on a new sense of purpose as people faced new environmental problems such as smog and toxic chemicals. Rachel Carson, Paul Ehrlich, Barry Commoner, and others sounded the alarm about pesticide poisoning, air and water pollution, overpopulation, and nuclear fallout; new environmental groups formed in answer to these alarms. Not to be left behind, the old-style conservation organizations shook off years of dormancy and, under a new generation of directors, burst into a flurry of activity that some called the "New Conservationism." Led by Howard Zahniser, the Wilderness Society began its long fight for the Wilderness Preservation Act. The Sierra Club, too, came dramatically alive, launching several highly visible campaigns that placed wilderness protection back on the list of vital environmental issues.

The Sierra Club's transformation from a genteel hiking club to a major force in environmental activism was mostly the work of a charismatic, combative, idealistic man named David Brower, who has been called "the environmental movement's high priest, its resident genius, patriarch, and bad boy rolled into one." Born in 1912, Brower grew up in Berkeley, California. One of his childhood pastimes was wandering in the hills east of San Francisco Bay with his blind mother; in describing the terrain to her, he learned to be observant and to use language skillfully. When Brower was 12 years old, he read John Muir's *My First Summer in the Sierra* and fell under the spell of the mountains. Shy and solitary, he dropped out of college after two years to haunt the Sierra Nevada, camping and climbing in Muir's old territory. Like Bob Marshall, founder of the Wilderness Society, Brower became a tireless mountaineer at a young age. Stephen Fox, author of *The American Wilderness Movement: John Muir and His Legacy*, reports that during the 1930s Brower scaled 33 Sierra peaks that had never before been climbed, once climbing three 14,000-footers in just 12 hours.

In 1933 Brower met Ansel Adams, a photographer and Sierra Club member, who sponsored Brower's entry into the club. Brower began leading Sierra Club wilderness expeditions. His shyness disappeared in the high country, and he captivated everyone with his enthusiasm, imagination, and puckish good humor. Brower became editor of the Sierra Club magazine in 1946, a member of the governing board in 1949, and the club's first full-time, salaried director in 1952. No sooner had Brower assumed leadership of the Sierra Club than he was presented with a cause around which to rally the conservationists and the American people.

The Bureau of Reclamation (BuRec), the federal agency responsible for water projects, announced ambitious plans to build a series of dams in the Colorado River basin to supply hydroelectric power to the Rocky Mountain states and the Southwest. Conservationists were horrified to learn that one of the proposed dam sites was in Echo Park, part of Dinosaur National Monument, a fossil-rich canyonland on the Colorado-Utah border. Not only would the dam flood the canyon but, as with the Hetch Hetchy dam 30 years earlier, its construction would mean that the protection supposedly granted by the National Park System was hollow. Zahniser of the Wilderness Society and Brower of the Sierra Club decided to fight BuRec; the National Audubon Society, the National Wildlife Federation, and the Izaak Walton League joined the fight.

Brower soon showed that he had a flair for smart public-relations gestures. He persuaded author Wallace Stegner, a friend and fellow conservationist, to edit a book called *This Is Dinosaur*, which was rushed into print and passed out to congresspeople and the media. He also performed brilliantly at congressional hearings, organized letter-writing campaigns, and used newspaper ads to turn the public against the dam—tactics that environmentalists had never before used on such a large scale, or so flamboyantly.

Muir had lost his fight to save Hetch Hetchy, but Brower, Zahniser, and the other conservationists won their battle. The Echo Park dam was never built, and today the Echo Park campaign is considered a landmark victory for the environmental movement. To some of the winners, though, the victory had a sour taste, for the conservationists had made a painful compromise. In return for the sparing of Echo Park, they had agreed not to fight the building of a dam in Glen Canyon, a wild canyon on Navajo land along the Arizona-Utah border. John Wesley Powell had explored the canyon and written of its haunting beauty, its strange geology, and its mysterious Native American relics. But when the Glen Canyon dam was built, the canyon was lost forever. Ironically, the reservoir created by the dam was named Lake Powell. Brower came to regret the deal that the conservationists had made. "Glen Canyon died in 1963," he wrote, "and I was partly responsible for its death." Since that time, Brower has scorned compromise and political deal-making; other environmentalists, however, feel that it is a sad reality that victories must be bought with trade-offs.

An even bigger storm blew up in the 1960s: BuRec wanted to build a dam in Grand Canyon National Monument. Brower took the lead in rallying the conservationists all over again. He produced a glossy new Sierra Club book on the Grand Canyon, and he paid for expensive, attention-getting ads in the nation's newspapers and magazines. "NOW ONLY YOU CAN STOP THE GRAND CANYON FROM BEING FLOODED . . . FOR PROFIT," shouted one ad, which concluded, "This time it's the Grand Canyon they want to flood. *The Grand Canyon.*" Another Sierra Club ad in the *New York Times* asked, "SHOULD WE FLOOD THE SISTINE CHAPEL SO TOURISTS CAN GET NEAR THE CEILING?" The shock tactics worked. Americans responded in record numbers, swamping congressional offices with angry telegrams, calls and letters. BuRec dropped its plan, and the new, high-powered Sierra Club was recognized as a leader in environmental activism. But the club's success was costly. The day after one of the club's most sensational ads appeared, the Internal Revenue Service (IRS) suspended the Sierra Club's tax-free status. Brower made sure that the IRS action received front-page media attention, and the club won considerable sympathy.

Under Brower's direction, the Sierra Club grew from 7,000 members in 1952 to 77,000 in 1969, becoming a national, rather than a local, organization. It sold $10 million dollars' worth of books, many of them containing Ansel Adams's extraordinary black-and-white photographs of Yosemite. Yet some club leaders, including Stegner and Adams, felt that Brower was a poor business manager and that he was running the Sierra Club as a one-man show, making too many decisions himself; Stegner said that Brower had been "bitten by the worm of power." After a long and bitter fight with his colleagues, Brower was forced out of the Sierra Club. He founded his own environmental group, Friends of the Earth (FOE), in 1970. Later, after disagreements with other FOE directors, he founded the Earth Island Institute in 1985. Brower also helped organize the League of Conservation Voters, which keeps track of how members of Congress vote on environmental bills.

Boyish and energetic into his eighties, the "high priest" of modern environmentalism has remained involved with various Earth Island projects. Brower's influence has been felt everywhere within the environmental movement. He has motivated or advised many of the leading conservationists, ecologists, and environmental activists. The pattern he set in the epic battles over Echo Park and the Grand Canyon, using big-budget advertising and the national media, is now standard practice for the Sierra Club and other high-profile environmental organizations when they have a cause to promote or an alarm to sound.

CHAPTER FIVE NOTES

page 52   "isolated and priestlike . . ." Quoted in *Paul Brooks,* **The House of Life: Rachel Carson at Work,** p. 128.

page 52   "Science is part . . ." *Paul Brooks,* **The House of Life: Rachel Carson at Work,** p. 129.

page 54   "For the first time . . ." *Rachel Carson,* **Silent Spring,** p. 15.

page 54   "to scare the American public . . ." Quoted in *Robert Gottlieb,* **Forcing the Spring: The Transformation of the American Environmental Movement,** p. 85.

page 56   "The miraculous succession . . ." *Fairfield Osborn,* **Our Plundered Planet,** p. 199.

page 57   "inexhaustible resource of technology" Quoted in *Robert Gottlieb,* **Forcing the Spring: The Transformation of the American Environmental Movement,** p. 37.

page 58   "The greatest need today . . ." *Paul Ehrlich and Anne Ehrlich,* **The Population Explosion,** p. 202.

page 59   "the enveloping cloud . . ." *Barry Commoner,* **Science and Survival,** p. 108.

page 60   "the environmental movement's high priest . . ." *Susan Zakin,* **Coyotes and Town Dogs: Earth First! and the Environmental Movement,** p. 151.

page 61   Brower's climbing feats in *Stephen Fox,* **The American Conservation Movement: John Muir and His Legacy,** p. 275.

page 62   "Glen Canyon died . . ." *David Brower,* **The Place No One Knew,** Quoted in *Susan Zakin,* **Coyotes and Town Dogs: Earth First! and the Environmental Movement,** p. 161.

page 63   "bitten by the worm . . ." Quoted in *Susan Zakin,* **Coyotes and Town Dogs: Earth First! and the Environmental Movement,** p. 169.

CHAPTER Six

THE CLEAN AND GREEN LAWS

The environmental movement owed much of its growth in the 1960s to the general social unrest that swept the nation during that turbulent decade. Many of today's committed environmentalists can trace the roots of their commitment to the late 1960s, when the youth counterculture that flourished in the colleges and universities urged, "Back to nature!" The counterculture sprang up as young people rebelled against what they saw as the stifling limitations of conventional society. They wore long hair and tie-dyed hippie clothing as badges of defiant individualism and listened to Jefferson Airplane, Pink Floyd, and other loud new rock bands. The counterculture rebellion took many forms; some, such as drug use, were far from benign. In other ways, though, the counterculture encouraged a healthy examination of social values. Environmental abuse was one of many aspects of society that young people began to criticize and reject.

During the 1960s, thousands of Americans joined the civil rights, antiwar, and women's movements. Through marches, demonstrations, boycotts—and sometimes more aggressive methods such as sit-ins or seizures of buildings—protesters demanded reform. And they got it. The Civil Rights Act was passed in 1964 because enough people had publicly insisted that the United States change the way it treated African Americans and other minorities. The U.S. began to withdraw from the Vietnam War at the end of the 1960s at least in part because of loud and relentless antiwar activity at home. These victories reminded Americans of their power to bring about change. One who believed that the time was ripe for environmental change was Gaylord Nelson, a Democratic senator and former governor of Wisconsin.

Nelson had read *Our Plundered Planet, A Sand County Almanac*, and *Silent Spring*. He believed that government should take a more urgent interest in environmental protection. "I had hoped that the politicans, the Presidents, and governors would start talking about the issue, but they never did," he later recalled. "The climate was there, though," Nelson said. In September of 1969, after meeting with Paul Ehrlich to talk about overpopulation, Nelson read a magazine article about teach-ins—activities organized by college students to spark discussion of the Vietnam War. Some teach-ins were outright protest demonstrations, but most took the form of day-long debates between students and teachers; sometimes people from the community were invited to take part. Nelson decided that what the United States needed was a national teach- in about the environment. Earth Day was born.

Nelson drummed up support from a few other members of Congress and hired Denis Hayes, a law student at Harvard University, to organize the event. They picked April 22, 1970 as the target date because it fell during a week when most colleges did not have exams or holidays. Absurdly, a few suspicious folk declared that Earth Day was a communist plot because April 22 was the birthday of V. I. Lenin, founder of Russian communism. One overexcited state official in Georgia spent $1,600 of the taxpayers' money on telegrams warning President Nixon and other lawmakers of the so-called communist plot; after annoyed taxpayers complained, he sheepishly repaid the money from his own pocket.

Meanwhile, Earth Day gathered momentum. Schools and service organizations announced plans to participate, and the media began reporting on the preparations. Sensing the public's growing concern about the environment, government and industry hastened to jump on the bandwagon. President Nixon made speeches about the need to control pollution and clean up the nation's air and water. Chemical and utility companies, hoping to improve their image in the eyes of environmentalists, sponsored events and donated money and equipment. No one who wanted to participate was discouraged. Hayes's goal was to make Earth Day as broad-based as possible, to attract everyone—especially middle-class, conservative Americans who disliked the aggressive, confrontational tactics of antiwar activists. Hayes tried to present Earth Day as a celebration, not a protest, although many of the events that unfolded were protests.

Not everyone was happy with the all-inclusive, broad-based approach to Earth Day. Although business and government leaders gave lip service to the idea, most of them remained deeply wary of the environmental movement. At the other end of the political spectrum, radical left-wing activists were angry to see business, government, and the mainstream media involved in Earth Day. They also felt that by focusing on fix-it approaches to surface issues such as pollution control and litter, the environmental movement was missing its chance to press for more basic reforms. Instead of negotiating for limits on how much soot or poison could be spewed from factory chimneys, for example, these activists wanted to ban fossil fuels and toxic chemicals altogether and remake society along the lines laid out by Murray Bookchin and Barry Commoner. Much closer to the mainstream, the Sierra Club and some of the other old-line conservation organizations also kept their distance from Earth Day, fearing that the new environmentalists, with their emphasis on pollution and toxic chemicals, would draw attention away from the more traditional issue of wilderness preservation. Yet the planners of Earth Day stuck with their moderate, "something for everyone" approach, believing that environmentalism had to widen its appeal in order to win successes like those of the civil rights movement.

Earth Day gave environmentalism a personal dimension. Individuals began to believe that they *could* make a difference. Parents whose children came home from school and talked about recycling began removing newspapers and bottles from their household trash for recycling. Teenagers whose classes had made field trips to landfills started campaigns against disposable plastic cups in their school cafeterias. Car pools sprang up as drivers acknowledged their contributions to air pollution. The idea that individual choices and actions could help solve environmental problems became part of the American consciousness.

The scope and scale of the first Earth Day surprised even its organizers. Historians of environmentalism agree that April 22, 1970 was a crucial event in modern environmental history. Earth Day brought the movement down to the grass roots and encouraged people to get involved. It motivated a tremendous number of people to join environmental organizations for the first time, swelling the ranks of the Audubon Society and other associations. It also demonstrated beyond doubt that the American people were concerned for the health of the environment. After Earth Day, environmental topics began appearing often in schools, the media, and legislative assemblies.

Earth Day brought the big environmental organizations not just new members but also new energy. In the years after the first Earth Day, new alliances were formed among environmentalists. Various groups—antinuclear and public-health activists, wilderness and wildlife preservationists, and pollution watchdogs—joined together to show strength in numbers and to support each other's causes. The environmental movement became broader and somewhat more unified. According to environmental historian Philip Shabecoff, "The principles of ecology, both scientific and moral, welded the old and the new environmentalism into a movement of fiercely competing but relatively unified national organizations." In fact, the terms *environmentalist* and *environmentalism* came into general use only in the 1970s. They suggested a broader concern than *conservationist* and *conservationism*, a concern that included toxic chemicals, waste disposal, overpopulation, and air and water quality as well as wildlife and wilderness.

The environmental ferment that found expression on Earth Day sparked a flurry of legislation as lawmakers scurried to respond to the concern shown by voters. It had become clear that industry and individuals, left to themselves, did not take care of the environment. This point was driven home by ecologist Garrett Hardin in a widely read essay called "The Tragedy of the Commons," which appeared in *Science* magazine in 1968. Hardin used the parable of a commons, which is a publicly owned pasture on which everyone in the community can graze cattle. Naturally, each individual cattle owner uses the commons as much as possible, because it is free. But because *all* the cattle owners let all their

By-products of the coal and steel industries fill the sky above Pittsburgh, Pennsylvania in 1905. Fifty years later, U.S. lawmakers took their first halting steps toward controlling air pollution. *(Library of Congress)*

animals graze on it all the time, the commons is soon stripped of grass, eroded, and no good to anyone.

Hardin's argument was that air, water, and public land are like the commons. If users, such as drivers whose cars expel waste into the air or cities that discharge sewage into the rivers, are not required to pay for the damage they do, they have no reason to limit their use or destruction of the public resources. Factories, for example, will not install costly pollution-control devices in their smokestacks just because it might be nice to keep the air a little cleaner—they must be compelled to do so by federal laws and fined if they break those laws. A minimum of care for the "commons" must be built into the ordinary operating cost of cars, furnaces, factories, utilities plants, and the like.

Well before Earth Day, the federal government had passed a few landmark environmental laws, notably the first Clean Air Act (1955) and the Wilderness Preservation Act (1964). But during the 1970s, reacting to the outpouring of public interest in the environment, Congress rolled up its sleeves and created a slew of new laws. In 1970, legislators passed the National Environmental Policy Act, which requires the government to report on how its activities affect the environment; the Occupational Safety and Health Act (OSHA), which protects people from toxic and dangerous substances in the workplace; the Solid Waste Disposal Act, aimed at bringing the nation's swelling landfills and garbage heaps under control; and a revised, stronger Clean Air Act. Also in 1970, Nixon created the Environmental Protection Agency (EPA) to see that the new laws were enforced.

More legislation followed. In 1972 Congress passed the Ocean Dumping Act to govern the disposal of wastes and other materials in U.S. waters; the Marine Mammal Protection Act to protect sea otters, seals, dolphins, and whales; the Federal Insecticide, Fungicide, and Rodenticide Act (FIFRA) to govern the use of pesticides; and the Federal Water Pollution Control Act, aimed at making all American waterways safe to swim and fish in by 1983. The Endangered Species Act—a key piece of legislation that was supposed to protect endangered species and their habitats—was passed in 1973, and the Safe Drinking Water Act was passed in 1974. In 1976, Congress passed the Toxic Substances Control Act (TOSCA) and the Resource Conservation and Recovery Act (RECRA), both of which govern the use and disposal of hazardous materials. Laws regulating air and water pollution were revised and strengthened in 1977. In 1980, Congress rounded out its decade of "green" lawmaking with the Alaska National Interest Lands Act, which set aside 100 million acres in Alaska for varying levels of environmental protection, and the Comprehensive Environmental Response, Compensation, and Liability Act (CERCLA), which created a financial Superfund to pay for cleanups at the worst of the nation's abandoned toxic waste dumps. In addition, the federal and state governments passed a host of lesser environmental laws during the 1970s, and millions of acres were added to the national parks, forests, and wildlife refuges.

This thicket of environmental legislation seemed to promise a clean, green America in the future. Has that promise been kept? Most observers agree that the environment is in better shape today than it would have been if the laws had never been passed—but not any better than it was in the late 1960s. Air quality has improved in some parts of the country, worsened in others. A number of rivers are considerably cleaner and safer than they were in 1970, but millions of acres of wetlands—ecosystems crucial not just to the life cycles of birds and fish but also to natural water-purification cycles—have been lost to development and pollution. Most Superfund sites remain highly toxic. The deadline for meeting air-quality standards set in 1970 has been repeatedly extended; the standards have never been met. Some petroleum processors, chemical manufacturers, and mining companies regluarly pay the relatively small fines charged to them under the regulations and continue to pollute. Congress has several times overturned efforts to protect wildlife and ecosystems under the Endangered Species Act.

These and other failures are partly the fault of the laws, many of which are complicated, clumsy, and inadequate. But the laws have failed to live up to their promise partly because of federal policy. Jimmy Carter, who was president of the United States from 1976 to 1980, believed in the need for environmental reform. In 1980, his Council on Environmental Quality published the Global 2000 Report, which stated that "if present trends continue, the world in 2000 will be more crowded, more polluted, less stable ecologically and more vulnerable to disruption than the world we know today." But Carter was succeeded as president by Ronald Reagan, who after two terms was succeeded by his vice-president, George Bush.

Both Reagan and Bush were far more sympathetic to industry, development, ranching, mining, and logging than to environmentalism. Their administrations slashed the budgets of the EPA and ended programs to develop alternative energy sources, such as solar and wind power. Reagan's secretary of the interior, James Watt, was a fundamentalist Christian who stated several times that conserving resources was not important because Jesus might return to Earth tomorrow, bringing the Day of Judgment. This impending event, however, evidently did not stand in the way of doing business. Backed by western coal, ranching, and hydroelectric interests, Watt embarked on large-scale plans to increase oil drilling, coal mining, and other economic activities on publicly owned lands. He showed little or no interest in enforcing the environmental laws.

The National Wildlife Federation and the Sierra Club gathered millions of signatures on petitions calling for Watt's resignation. Too outrageous even for the Reagan administration, Watt was forced to resign in 1983. Donald Hodel, secretary of the interior for most of the rest of Reagan's administration, was not much of an improvement, in the opinion of environmentalists. One of his more memorable statements concerned the damage done by industrial chemicals to the ozone layer of the Earth's atmosphere, which shields the planet's surface from harmful ultraviolet rays. Hodel said that replacing the destructive chemicals would be troublesome and costly, and that the problem would be solved if everyone would just wear sunglasses, sun lotion, and hats. Hodel may have intended his remark as a joke, but it was seized upon by reporters and environmentalists as a mark of his unfitness for his job.

Anne Gorsuch, named by Reagan to head the EPA, was another regulator more interested in the exploitation than the preservation of public lands and resources. Her top advisors were lawyers and executives from the chemical, automobile, and petroleum industries. Her disregard for the regulations she was supposed to enforce was so glaring that Congress began investigating the EPA in 1982. Investigators discovered that top EPA officials had made improper deals with companies concerning Superfund cleanup sites. Gorsuch was pressured into resigning in 1983, and one of her top aides went to jail for six months for lying to Congress. A decade later, the EPA had not yet regained its morale, its muscle, or its credibility. Many environmentalists are convinced that the EPA can never be anything but a political agency that will do whatever the current administration wants. In 1990, environmentalist Jon Naar summed up the state of the agency in *Design for a Livable Planet:* "Although EPA enforcement has improved from the nadir reached during the bad old days of Anne Gorsuch, it is still inadequate and the environmental laws remain as much promise as reality."

During the 1980s, the government's backlash against environmentalism was matched in corporate America—except for the fast-growing pollution-control industry, which by 1992 was doing an estimated $125 billion worth of business each year. Complaints about the difficulty of obeying the new regulations and about environmental extremism appeared more and more often in business publications and in the messages spread by lobbyists for industry. The chemical industry was especially eager to convince the Reagan administration and the general public that the dangers of cancer-causing toxic chemicals had been grossly overstated. This point of view was expressed in journalist Edith Efron's 1984 book *The Apocalyptics: Cancer and the Big Lie,* which

Anne Gorsuch headed the Environmental Protection
Agency from 1980 to 1983, a period of
antienvironmentalism in the federal government. She filled
top positions in the EPA with people from big
business—letting the foxes guard the henhouse,
complained environmentalists. (*Library of Congress*)

The Clean and Green Laws   **73**

said that contrary to the claims of environmentalists and many medical experts, pesticides and other chemicals did not cause cancer in humans. Efron accused Rachel Carson, Barry Commoner, Paul Ehrlich, the National Cancer Institute, and others of spreading unnecessary alarm. Environmentalists' fears, she said, were based not on science but on a "Carsonian religion."

In some ways, Efron was right. Environmentalism has always been driven as much by passion and conviction as by science and common sense. Many environmentalists, including John Muir, Rachel Carson, and millions of ordinary people, have felt a spiritual connection with the natural world and a sacred duty to protect it—much like the sense of inspired duty that has motivated Gandhi, Martin Luther King, and other civil rights activists. And it is true that the facts, figures, and arguments put forward by environmentalists have sometimes been shaky. But the same has been true, many times, of the facts and figures marshaled against environmentalists by chemical industry scientists or real estate developers.

People often think of "science" as a single, objective truth, but science is actually a continual process of inquiry and investigation. Like statistics, science can be made to serve many masters, depending upon who is paying the bill. It is now well established that many industrial chemicals do indeed cause increased rates of cancer in people who are exposed to them. Environmentalists, whose ranks include hundreds of distinguished scientists, are confident that the weight of the scientific evidence supports their position on a wide range of other issues as well. They are certainly motivated by feelings and beliefs—as are corporate executives and legislators, for that matter—but they want the solutions to environmental problems to be based on well-informed consideration of the best available science, not on politics or economics. America's environmental laws, however, were shaped as much by the politics of compromise as by science. They are a step in the right direction, say environmentalists, but they do not go far enough.

CHAPTER SIX NOTES

page 66   "I had hoped . . ." Quoted in *Philip Shabecoff,* **A Fierce Green Fire: The American Environmental Movement,** p. 114.

page 68   "The principles of ecology . . ." *Philip Shabecoff,* **A Fierce Green Fire: The American Environmental Movement,** p. 120.

page 71   "if present trends continue . . ." Quoted in *Philip Shabecoff,* **A Fierce Green Fire: The American Environmental Movement,** p. 203.

page 72   "Although EPA enforcement has improved . . ." *Jon Naar,* **Design for a Livable Planet,** p. 242.

"THINK GLOBALLY, ACT LOCALLY"

In the early 1970s, the U.S. government had seemed ready to lead the world in environmental reform. By the end of that decade, it had dropped the ball. During the administrations of Ronald Reagan and George Bush (1980–1992), the federal commitment to environmental reform wavered both at home and abroad. At home, the government slashed EPA funds, continued to build highways at the expense of energy-saving public transit systems, openly ignored its own regulations when storing toxic nuclear waste at weapons plants, abandoned efforts to develop renewable and environmentally safe energy sources, and permitted vast increases in timber clearcutting and wetlands development. Abroad, the United States withdrew funding from population-control programs, continued to manufacture hazardous chemicals and dispose of toxic wastes in Third World countries, and lagged behind other nations in opposition to rainforest burning, drift-net deep-sea fishing—in which enormous numbers of sea mammals and birds are killed by the long nets that strip the seas of edible fish—and other destructive practices.

Yet although environmentalism lost momentum in government, it remained important to many Americans. The major environmental organizations kept growing, many of them forming new regional, state, or local chapters. By 1993, the Sierra Club had

580,000 members and 350 local groups; the Wilderness Society had 300,000 members; the National Wildlife Federation was sending *Ranger Rick* and other educational publications to more than a million children each month; and the National Audubon Society had 560,000 members and 512 local chapters. A 1989 Gallup poll found that 75 percent of Americans described themselves as environmentalists (of course, "I'm an environmentalist" can mean anything from "I like nature shows on TV" to "I block bulldozers with my body").

Ecologist and biologist René Dubos (1900–1982), known for his discovery of new antibiotic drugs during World War II, gave much thought to the direction society was taking. Dubos was disturbed by what he called the "chaos in the relationships between man and his environment." He coined a phrase that has become a slogan of the environmental movement: "Think Globally, Act Locally." By "thinking globally," Dubos meant realizing that many environmental problems are global in scope because the Earth is one huge, interconnected ecological system. By "acting locally," he meant that individuals must do what is within their reach, and that people can be surprisingly effective at solving problems in their own communities.

Dubos's slogan neatly summarizes the two directions taken by the American environmental movement in recent years. In the early 1970s, the movement operated primarily on the national scale, through large national organizations and federal legislation. By the late 1970s, the movement had begun to spiral outward in two directions: Environmentalism went global, or international, and at the same time it became a local, grass-roots phenomenon.

The global perspective is represented by the World Wildlife Fund (WWF), the U.S. branch of the international WWF family, which includes organizations from several dozen nations that have joined together to protect wildlife and wildlands around the world. As its symbol, the WWF chose China's easily recognized, endangered panda. The appealing black-and-white creature has become familiar to millions of Americans, who have also taken an impassioned interest in the plight of the Siberian tiger, the Himalayan snow leopard, baby seals, various species of whales, and the African elephant and mountain gorilla. (Ecologists caution, however, that although the emphasis on large, recognizable, "likable"

The panda is a symbol not just of the World Wildlife Fund, one of the world's largest environmental organizations, but also of Americans' growing interest in global ecology. *(Jesse Cohen, National Zoological Park, Smithsonian Institution)*

mammals may drum up support for wildlife protection, critters less immediately attractive to the general public—such as dung beetles, hyenas, or krill—should not be overlooked. It will not do much good to save the whales, for example, if the krill they live on is stripped from the seas by factory ships for use as pet food and fertilizer.)

Since the 1970s, American environmental organizations and scientific research teams have been forging links with groups in other countries. The Nature Conservancy's "Parks in Peril" program hopes to save 200 nature parks in Latin America by the year 2000. The Audubon Society has been working with the nations of Central and South America to preserve sanctuaries for birds whose annual migrations carry them from the Arctic to the equator. The WWF monitors the illegal international trade in endangered plants, birds, and animals and works with law-enforcement agencies in many countries to halt the traffic.

Wildlife protection is not the only environmental issue now being confronted at the international level. Some of the most pressing problems, including global warming, waste disposal, and ozone damage, demand global solutions. "Acid rain knows no borders," say environmentalists, pointing to lakes in Canada and Sweden that have been killed by pollution from thousands of miles away. Nuclear contamination knows no borders, either, as Europeans and Russians discovered in 1985, when an explosion at the Chernobyl nuclear reactor in the Ukraine dusted the continent with radioactive fallout. Water-borne pollution or trash also stubbornly refuses to stay where it has been dumped. Oil slicks from tanker spills have been known to travel hundreds of miles, and syringes and lab samples have bobbed up on beaches far from where hospital waste was thrown into the ocean.

Experts in global politics are beginning to agree with environmentalists that ecological crises could lead to international disputes, possibly even to war. In the decades ahead, as overcrowding increases and resources dwindle, nations may fight over water rights or petroleum deposits; ecological problems are already contributing to tension in places like sub-Saharan Africa, where drought, famine, and the spread of the desert have created thousands of "eco-refugees." In 1988, Mikhail Gorbachev, the last president of the Soviet Union, warned of the growing need for "ecological security." After overseeing the end of the Soviet Union, Gorbachev became president of Green Cross, an international environmental group, declaring, "We need a global focus.

We can't build an ecologically safe future unless nations work together."

"Thinking globally" has become a lot easier with the advent of personal computers and electronic networking. Simply by sitting in front of a properly equipped computer, American environmentalists and scientists can share information and ideas with colleagues all over the world through electronic mail or on-line conferences. EcoNet is one of several computer networks for environmentalists. It links ecologists and activists on five continents, monitors environmental crises and legislative action, and has a bulletin board with topics ranging from "Antarctica" to "zoos." Such networks may become the leading environmental organizations of the future.

While American environmentalists were learning to think globally, they were also learning to act locally. They learned an important lesson about the power of local action in the 1960s, when a struggle in New York's Hudson River Valley showed them how to use the courts to protect the scenic value of the environment. Consolidated Edison, the local electric company, wanted to build a power plant on top of Storm King Mountain. Hikers and campers who treasured the area's beauty objected. So did a number of other local citizens, who felt that the proposed plant was unnecessary and would be an eyesore. They formed a grass-roots group—a local citizens' association—called the Scenic Hudson Preservation Conference (SHPC). The SHPC hired lawyers and sued the Federal Power commission for denying citizens the right to block the project. The commission complained that the SHPC could not sue because the citizens had not been physically or financially injured. The court, however, decided that the SHPC had the right to sue to protect the "aesthetic, conservational, or recreational" qualities of Storm King Mountain. The court ordered Consolidated Edison to consider alternatives to building the plant. In the end, the utility company dropped the idea altogether.

The Storm King case was an environmental landmark, for two reasons. First, the SHPC showed what ordinary people could accomplish in their own communities if they were willing to share the effort and expense of fighting industry. Second, by deciding that environmental values such as scenic and recreational qualities could be defended under the law, the court gave the movement one of its most powerful tools. Since then, environmental lawsuits in the thousands have been filed by individuals, communities, activist associations, and large groups such as the Sierra Club, which in 1971 created an independent arm called the Sierra Club Legal Defense Fund to handle courtroom battles.

David Sive, a New York City attorney who represented the SHPC in the Storm King case, claims that the environmental movement has used lawsuits and the courts "as no other social movement before or since." In 1970, Sive and other lawyers who were interested in environmental issues founded the Natural Resources Defense Council (NRDC), which they called "a law firm for the environment." The NRDC provides legal assistance and advice for grass-roots activists. It also sponsors scientific research and public education on environmental issues; among its victories was a publicity campaign that drove the pesticide Alar off the market.

Courtroom fights over environmental values reflected the new breed of environmental activism that gained strength during the 1970s and 1980s. Called "grass-roots environmentalism" or "alternative environmentalism," it was local, based in neighborhoods and towns. The new breed of environmentalism had few, if any, ties with large mainstream groups such as the Sierra Club and the Audubon Society. Sometimes the grass-roots activists were concerned with protecting local wetlands or other natural sites, as in the Storm King case, but far more often they were motivated by fears about health and safety. They fought to keep toxic wastes, nuclear reactors, and hazardous-waste incinerators out of their communities. To these activists, environmentalism was a matter of everyday life and death.

Lois Gibbs is perhaps the best-known of the grass-roots environmental activists. In 1974, Gibbs, her husband, and her baby son moved into a pleasant working-class neighborhood in Niagara Falls, New York. A canal had been dug there decades earlier and then had been used as a dump for more than 30 years. The army, the city of Niagara Falls, and several chemical companies had dumped more than 200 different chemical compounds into Love Canal, as the old channel was called; at least a dozen of these compounds are now known to cause cancer and other diseases in

Grass-roots environmentalism with a touch of Hollywood: NIMBY activist Lois Gibbs and actor Ed Begley Jr. prepare to lead a march against toxic waste dumping. *(Courtesy of the Citizens Clearinghouse for Hazardous Waste)*

humans. Then the channel was filled in, and houses and an elementary school were built on top of it.

Lois Gibbs knew nothing of all this; she was a contented housewife. As she said later, "I had the picket fence, I had the swingset. I had the mortgage. . . . It was literally the American dream in every aspect of what society perceives the American dream to be." Until 1978, that is, when her son became seriously ill with asthma, epileptic seizures, and a blood disease. A daughter born in the Love Canal neighborhood also developed a blood disease. Around the same time, Gibbs began hearing rumors of strange fluids seeping through neighbors' basement walls. Then she read a newspaper article about the old canal and the chemicals that had been dumped there, and she made a connection: Her neighborhood was built on toxic wastes, and the wastes were making her children sick.

She went to the school and to the city. Officials dismissed her as a hysterical housewife. She decided to see if she could muster enough support to make them take her seriously. She did the only thing she could think of—she went from door to door, asking questions. "I was afraid a lot of doors would be slammed in my face, that people would think I was some crazy fanatic," she admitted. "But I did it anyway." She was appalled to discover that her community had abnormally high rates of birth defects, miscarriages, and diseases such as leukemia and other forms of cancer. She persuaded other residents to join her in a community group, the Love Canal Homeowners Association (LCHA), to bring their problem to someone's attention.

Gibbs's awakening as an activist occurred when she realized that no one—not local health officials, not the governor, not the EPA, not even the president—wanted to listen or help. Again and again, the LCHA was turned away or given the runaround. Gibbs and her colleagues became militant, staging press conferences, protest marches, and other events to get attention from public officials and the media. They burst in on meetings of state legislators. They marched outside the governor's office. Once 500 of them surrounded a house where two EPA officials were visiting, keeping the officials hostage for hours. In 1980, under growing pressure from the national media and the LCHA, the federal government finally agreed to pay $17 million to move 900 families from the area. Gibbs had made "Love Canal" notorious as a symbol of industrial waste gone wild; one angry city official grumbled that the public viewed Niagara Falls as "the environmental Hiroshima."

The government cleaned up the toxic waste, and in 1988 people started moving back into Love Canal, now called Black Creek Village. Lois Gibbs, however, had moved on to Virginia, where she founded an organization called the Citizens Clearinghouse for Hazardous Waste (CCHW). During the battle over Love Canal, Gibbs had received hundreds of calls and letters from people all over the country, telling her of environmental disasters in their communities. She was seen as a heroine for having fought successfully against government and corporate indifference. People asked her how to organize local groups like the LCHA: the CCHW was her response. Since 1981 the organization has worked with thousands of grass-roots groups, providing scientific information, ideas on how to organize groups, and suggestions for action. It also puts small groups in touch with one another so that they can combine forces throughout a state or region. Slender, dark-haired, and intense, Gibbs has crisscrossed the country to meet with environmental groups and lead protest marches. The woman who once suffered from nervous nausea for three days before she could get up the courage to knock on the first door in her neighborhood has grown into a tough, effective speaker who uses her own experience to prove that ordinary citizens possess extraordinary power.

Lois Gibbs and Love Canal became models for other activists and communities who have protested against what they feel are dangers to their homes and families. Most of their targets have involved pollution and hazardous substances: toxic chemical dumps, landfills, incinerators to burn hazardous waste (which release toxic emissions into the air), and nuclear power plants (which involve the storage of radioactive wastes as well as the threat of a radiation leak). Activists have lobbied to close down existing facilities and to keep new ones from being built.

The antinuclear movement has spawned many vehement and effective grass-roots organizations. In the 1970s, citizens opposed

Eight protesters hoping to halt construction of the Seabrook nuclear plant stage a sit-in on the White House lawn in 1977. *(Library of Congress)*

the building of a nuclear reactor at Seabrook, New Hampshire. When lawsuits and lobbying by the community failed to halt the project, frustrated activists united in the Clamshell Alliance, taking their name from the clam-rich local waters. They adopted the direct-action approach, modeling their strategy on an antinuclear protest in Germany in which 28,000 protesters had occupied a site and prevented a plant from being built. The Clamshell Alliance worked with a smaller number, however: Only 18 activists turned out for the first occupation of the Seabrook site. The next sit-in drew 180, and in April of 1977 2,400 antinuclear activists occupied the site in an act of criminal trespass that they viewed as a moral necessity. They attracted national media attention with slogans such as "Better Active Today than Radioactive Tomorrow," and they also took their message to the nation's capital with marches and sit-ins at the White House.

The Clamshell Alliance served as a model for other antinuclear groups, including the Abalone Alliance, a coalition of environmentalists, peace activists, and concerned local citizens who mounted large-scale protests against the building of a reactor at Diablo Canyon, California; 40,000 people showed up for one Abalone Alliance rally. Both the Seabrook and the Diablo Canyon reactors were eventually built, although the protesters caused significant delays and postponements. But the activists had shown communities how to unite against unwanted nuclear technology. Protests by local groups have succeeded in blocking other projects and in shutting down reactors in Rancho Seco, California, and Shoreham, New York. Grass-roots antinuclear groups receive support, information, and advice through networks such as the Nuclear Information and Resource Service of Washington, D.C., and Critical Mass, which is part of Public Citizen, a Washington, D.C. organization founded by consumer advocate Ralph Nader.

Grass-roots activism of the sort practiced by Lois Gibbs and the Clamshell Alliance has come to be called the NIMBY movement—for Not In My Back Yard. Critics of NIMBY groups call them selfish, claiming that waste and power plants have to go somewhere, and that by saying "Not in *my* backyard," communities are simply passing the problem on to someone else. NIMBY activists disagree. "Why do we *have* to have poisonous waste and air pollution at all?" they challenge. They want everyone to take up the fight, so that "Not in my backyard" becomes "Not in anyone's backyard."

For the NIMBY activists, the key issue is participation. They are tired of corporations and government agencies that put potentially dangerous facilities in communities without consulting the people who will live next door to the landfills, smokestacks, and reactors. "No one asked our opinion, no one included us in the process," says Gary Murray, who organized a protest against a trash incinerator in his Maryland community. "We felt we needed to be part of the process." The grass-roots environmentalists are demanding a more participatory, more democratic kind of decision making.

Most NIMBYs have operated without any help from mainstream environmental organizations such as the Sierra Club and the National Wildlife Federation. Many NIMBY activists feel that the big groups, while effective in their way, are primarily concerned with broad issues such as wilderness and wildlife preservation and do not have much to offer in the day-to-day fight against local polluters. The NIMBYs can be sharply critical of the mainstream groups; for example, a Vermont CCHW activist challenged the National Wildlife Federation after learning that the chairman of Waste Management, Inc., a company notorious as one of the country's worst toxic polluters, had been named to the NWF's board of directors.

In terms of gender, race, and economic status, the NIMBY movement differs dramatically from the big-name environmental groups. The staffs of the national groups are, as environmental historian Philip Shabecoff points out, "mostly white, well-educated, relatively affluent middle-class professionals." A large proportion of the top staffers and directors are men. As a legacy from the early days of the conservation movement, membership in these groups remains tilted toward people who have the time and money to travel, camp and backpack, pay membership dues, buy publications, and contribute to fund drives. Members of the national mainstream groups are generally liberal in their political views. They tend to come from the middle or upper-middle economic classes.

The NIMBY groups, on the other hand, represent a much broader economic, racial, educational, and political cross section of the American population. Many grass-roots activists and group organizers—almost certainly a majority of them—are women. People of color and people from working-class and low-income communities are heavily involved in grass-roots environmentalism, reacting to what they perceive as environmental injustice. As they point out, no one ever proposes to build a toxic waste incinerator next to a country club or in an affluent white suburb, but an unfairly large share of the nation's hazardous substances, garbage, polluting industries, and power plants fall into poor rural or inner-city neighborhoods. "They always put them in poor people's back yards," says Lois Gibbs. "Never in rich people's. Every community should have the right to choose. That's environmental justice."

Environmental justice, part of the larger issue of social justice, has received increased attention since the mid-1980s. In 1984, the Urban Environment Conference reported that ethnic and racial minorities were exposed to higher-than-average risks from toxic substances, both in the workplace and in their communities. This finding was echoed in 1986 by a government study prepared for the Congressional Black Caucus; the study found that treatment plants for hazardous waste tended to be located in crowded, poor districts with minority populations. In 1987, the United Church of Christ's Commission for Racial Justice exposed evidence of "environmental racism," revealing that "African Americans, Hispanic Americans, Asian Americans, and Native Americans disproportionately lived in communities with a dangerous concentration of hazardous waste sites. And, in 10 major metropolitan areas, more than 90 percent of African Americans lived in areas with uncontrolled waste sites." Black legislators are well aware of the link between race and environmental abuse. According to the League of Conservation Voters, the Congressional Black Caucus has a better voting record on environmental issues than any other group in Congress.

Some of the NIMBY movement's most heartening victories have occurred in poor or minority communities where people have banded together to fight for protection from environmental risks. As early as 1965, for example, community leaders in a black neighborhood in West Chicago, concerned about the health risks to their children from the lead-based paint found in much substandard housing, formed the Citizens Committee to End Lead Poisoning, which sparked the formation of similar groups in other cities. Eventually, pressure from these groups forced federal and civic agencies to ban lead-based paint and start removing it from existing buildings. In the 1980s, poor African Americans, Native Americans, and whites in Robeson County, North Carolina—a community with a history of racial discord—united in a grass-roots campaign that kept toxic-chemical and nuclear-waste processing plants from being built in their county.

Local and community activists often complain about the huge gap between the mainstream national environmental groups, which have the resources and the clout to command public and media attention, and the people who are most affected by environmental ills. In 1990, activist associations from Louisiana and New Mexico, both made up largely of people of color, wrote to the Sierra Club, the Audubon Society, and the other top ten national environmental organizations, criticizing the "racism and 'whiteness' of the environmental movement." The activists challenged the ten groups to add people of color to their staffs and boards of directors and to become more involved in the issues of social and environmental justice.

In response, officials of the Environmental Defense Committee and other mainstream groups admitted that they had done a terrible job of reaching out to minorities. Jay Hair of the National Wildlife Federation, an organization often criticized for its ties to business, said, "I don't think anybody is as aware of the whiteness of the green movement as those of us who are trying to do something about it." In a flurry of planning meetings and press releases, the mainstream groups announced a newfound commitment to multiethnic hiring and environmental justice, but they have yet to translate their pledges into action. Some NIMBY activists doubt that the national groups will really make significant changes.

But a few observers of the environmental movement have concluded that if the traditional groups want to remain effective, they will have to ally themselves with the local activists who are fighting for environmental justice. The NIMBY phenomenon and the environmental justice movement may define the future of American environmentalism. Estimates of the number of Americans who belong to environmental organizations vary widely, but the total may be as high as 25 million. Whatever the tally, however, the majority of members belong not to the big national organizations but to local, grass-roots groups. These grass-roots activists are broadening the definition of "environmentalist." In the process, they are discovering their own power. Al Gore, a former U.S. senator and President Bill Clinton's vice president, called the NIMBY movement "an undeniably powerful political force." In the years ahead, local action may be the most powerful force for environmental reform in America.

CHAPTER SEVEN NOTES

page 77   "chaos in the relationships . . ." *René Dubos,* **So Human an Animal,** p. 16.

page 79   "We need a global focus . . ." Interviewed by *Colin Greer,* "'The Well-Being of the World Is at Stake,'" **Parade**, January 23, 1994, p. 4.

page 81   "as no other social movement . . ." Tom Turner, "The Legal Eagles," in *Peter Borelli* (editor), **Crossroads,** p. 52.

page 81   "a law firm for the environment" Quoted in *Robert Gottlieb,* **Forcing the Spring: The Transformation of the American Environmental Movement,** p. 142.

page 82   "I had the picket fence . . ." Quoted in *Philip Shabecoff,* **A Fierce Green Fire: The American Environmental Movement,** p. 234.

page 83   "I was afraid . . ." Quoted in *Michael Vitez,* "Backyard Power," **Philadelphia Inquirer** magazine, November 29, 1992, p. 28.

page 83   "the environmental Hiroshima" *Michael Vitez,* "Backyard Power," **Philadelphia Inquirer** magazine, November 29, 1992, p. 28.

page 86   "No one asked . . ." Quoted in *Jon Naar,* **Design for a Livable Planet,** p. 276.

page 86   "mostly white, well-educated . . ." *Philip Shabecoff,* **A Fierce Green Fire: The American Environmental Movement,** p. 233.

page 87   "They always put them . . ." *Michael Vitez,* "Backyard Power," **Philadelphia Inquirer** magazine, p. 29.

page 87   "environmental racism . . . African Americans . . ." Commission for Racial Justice, quoted in *Philip Shabecoff,* **A Fierce Green Fire: The American Environmental Movement,** p. 241.

page 88   "racism and 'whiteness' . . ." Quoted in *Robert Gottlieb,* **Forcing the Spring: The Transformation of the American Environmental Movement,** p. 260.

page 88   "I don't think anybody . . ." Quoted in *Robert Gottlieb,* **Forcing the Spring: The Transformation of the American Environmental Movement,** p. 261.

page 89   "an undeniably powerful . . ." *Al Gore,* **Earth in the Balance: Ecology and the Human Spirit,** p. 355.

CHAPTER Eight

THE ECO-WARRIORS

Every major reform movement has spoken with many voices. A movement's overall goal may be large and seemingly simple: "Protect the environment!" or "Rights for women!" or "End racial discrimination!" But people within the movement may have many different ideas about how to proceed and what is most important.

Sometimes a reform movement is unified only in its opposition to everyone else; within the movement, factions may disagree and even fight with one another. In particular, conflict often arises over the issue of "working within the system." One faction of a movement believes that the best way to change things is to educate people, to build a broad base of support through lobbying and communication, and to win victories within the existing social and political system, in courtrooms, voting booths, and congressional committees. But another faction argues that there is no time for slow, gradual change, or that victories in the political arena are too watered down by compromise to be useful. This faction, usually a smaller or fringe element of the movement, may take a more radical approach and turn to direct action.

One form of direct action that environmentalists have used is civil disobedience: refusing to obey a law or a government authority. Civil disobedience may involve deliberate law-breaking, but it is nonviolent. For example, protesters may illegally occupy private property, such as a nuclear plant site, but they will not forcibly resist when arrested, and they will not use violence against others. Civil disobedience has a distinguished history. Thoreau was exercising civil disobedience when he went to jail rather than pay taxes to fund a war he believed was immoral. Gandhi and his followers used civil disobedience—massive marches, sit-ins, and strikes—to win India's independence from British rule. Martin Luther King and other American civil rights leaders used large-scale civil disobedience to call society's attention to their cause and to prod the government into passing laws against discrimination. Peace movements in the United States and elsewhere have also made much use of civil disobedience.

Environmentalists in the United States have used civil disobedience against nuclear power, pollution, and toxic waste. Since the 1960s, thousands of demonstrators have been arrested for assembling on the sites of existing or proposed nuclear power plants and hazardous-waste dumps. These acts of civil disobedience were generally the work of local residents or NIMBY groups. Civil disobedience sometimes takes the form of dramatic, attention-getting episodes in the "guerrilla theater" tradition, as when a group of local activists called the Eco-Commando Force poured yellow dye into a sewage-treatment plant in Dade County, Florida on Earth Day 1970. The "ecological commandos" made their point the following day, when boating canals and waterways throughout the area turned yellow, proving that the plant was not properly processing the sewage it discharged into local waters.

One of the world's largest and best-known environmental organizations started as an antinuclear direct-action group. In 1971 a group of Canadian environmentalists from Vancouver, British Columbia, came together to fight nuclear testing in Alaska's Aleutian Islands and elsewhere in the North Pacific Ocean. They took the name Greenpeace and modeled their tactics of nonviolent resistance on those used by Gandhi and King. Greenpeace hoped to do two things: to call public attention to the tests, and to halt them—if necessary, by putting their own lives at risk by sailing into the test zones. They took a small fishing boat north to Amchitka, the Aleutian island where the U.S. military planned to conduct underground tests of nuclear weapons.

Greenpeace did not make it into the test zone or stop that Amchitka test, but the group did get international publicity. More than 20,000 antinuclear demonstrators rallied at the U.S.–Canada border in support of the Greenpeace mission. Public pressure eventually halted testing on Amchitka, which later became a bird sanctuary. The voyage launched Greenpeace into environmental fame. Greenpeace branches quickly formed in other countries, including the United States.

Greenpeace's fight against nuclear testing continued. With cameras rolling, small ships—or sometimes just rubber rafts with outboard motors—doggedly churned into waters that had been restricted for weapons testing, where they confronted French and American military ships. Images of the tiny Greenpeace vessels and the valiant protesters were flashed around the world. Meanwhile, Greenpeace was broadening its scope. After encountering whales on their missions, the activists vowed to protect the huge, gentle sea mammals, which at the time were being slaughtered in the thousands by whaling ships from many nations. Greenpeace ships followed the whaling fleets, and volunteers in rubber dinghies placed themselves between the whales and the whalers' high-powered harpoon guns. Naturally, Greenpeace's attentions were not welcomed by the whalers, who sometimes sprayed the activists with high-pressure hoses. Greenpeace's daring escapades received worldwide attention and helped bring about international treaties against whale hunting; most nations—but not all—now abide by these agreements.

Other sea creatures came under Greenpeace's protection. The group received enormous publicity for its campaign to prevent the clubbing of baby seals for their fur. Accompanied by celebrities such as actress Brigitte Bardot, an animal-rights activist, protesters took to the rocky shores and ice floes of Labrador, Canada, hurling themselves between seal pups and seal hunters; they also dyed the pups' fur to make it worthless to the hunters. Greenpeace mounted other campaigns, for sea turtles and dolphins and against things that destroy the oceans and oceanic life: hazardous wastes, oil spills, and drift nets, the 35-to-40-mile-long nets that catch and kill not just food fish but birds, sea mammals, and everything in their path.

Greenpeace's firm opposition to nuclear testing brought the group into tragic conflict with the French military, which was conducting underground tests in French Polynesia in the South Pacific Ocean. In 1985, agents of the French secret service blew up the Greenpeace vessel *Rainbow Warrior* while it was docked in New Zealand, killing a photographer aboard the ship. If the agents' plan was to stop Greenpeace, it backfired. The incident outraged the New Zealand government and earned France stern protests from many governments and organizations around the world; it also led to an outpouring of support for Greenpeace.

In its early days, Greenpeace was a "fringe" group focused on direct, media-grabbing action. Greenpeace activists captured the reporter's camera and the public's eye with high-risk missions and imaginative stunts. Many stunts involved surprisingly placed banners. When the Statue of Liberty in New York harbor was being renovated, Greenpeacers sneaked up the scaffolding and astonished New Yorkers by unfurling a huge banner that read "Give Me Liberty From Nuclear Weapons." On another occasion, when a garbage barge made the news because it could not find a port that would accept its unpleasant load, Greenpeace activists draped the barge with a banner saying "Next Time, Try Recycling." Robert Hunter, one of the founders of Greenpeace, wrote in 1979, "If crazy stunts were required to draw the focus of the cameras that led back into millions and millions of brains, then crazy stunts were what we would do." In 1988, the *New York Times Magazine* labeled Greenpeacers "Daredevils for the Environment."

By 1993, Greenpeace had become one of the leading environmental organizations in the world, with offices in 150 countries and nearly two million contributors worldwide. Greenpeace runs EnviroNet, an international computer network for ecological issues, and attracts celebrity support; rock stars Sting, R.E.M., the Grateful Dead, and U2 appeared on a fund-raising album called *Rainbow Warriors*. In addition to its antinuclear stance and its guardianship of the sea, Greenpeace also campaigns for ozone protection, alternative energy sources, and environmental protection for Antarctica. Nonviolent direct action is still one of Greenpeace's tools, but it has been supplemented by mail campaigns, political lobbying, and research programs. With its large staff and big budget, Greenpeace has grown closer to the mainstream environmental organizations. Its place at the far fringe of environmentalism has been taken by other, more radical groups.

Paul Watson with a friend on the Canadian ice after the *Sea Shepherd,* at anchor in the background, had disrupted a 1983 seal hunt. *(Courtesy of the Sea Shepherd Conservation Society)*

One of those groups is headed by a passionate, controversial activist named Paul Watson. Born in Canada in 1950, Watson showed a strong interest in wildlife and animal welfare throughout his childhood. He also became aware at an early age of the damage done by humans to the natural world: "When I was a teenager," he has said, "I often wished that there had been people a century before who had fought for the survival of the buffalo, the Passenger pigeon, the Eastern timber wolf. Unfortunately there were none." Watson took to the sea in his teens and served on merchant ships, yachts, and Canadian Coast Guard vessels in many parts of the world. He was a founding member of Greenpeace and was part of the group's Amchitka mission. In 1977, during a campaign to save baby seals, Watson was kicked out of Greenpeace for breaking the group's pledge of nonviolence—he seized a club from a hunter and threw it into the sea. By that time, however, Watson was ready to part from Greenpeace. Its passive methods, he felt, simply did not go far enough.

Watson formed a group called Earthforce to investigate poaching of African elephants by ivory hunters. A year later, in 1978, with a ship donated by author and animal-rights activist Cleveland Amory, Watson changed his group's name to the Sea Shepherd Conservation Society and became an environmental vigilante on the high seas. In this role he has not hesitated to enforce marine-life treaties when he has seen them violated. Watson's tactics are more extreme than those of Greenpeace; although his operations have never caused a death or an injury, they have involved sabotage and violence against property.

In 1979, Watson's ship, the *Sea Shepherd*, rammed and disabled an illegal whaling ship called the *Sierra*; ordered by a Portuguese court to turn the *Sea Shepherd* over to the *Sierra*'s owners for use as a whaler, Watson sank his own ship and then scuttled the *Sierra*. Over the next decade, Sea Shepherd operations included sinking half of the Spanish and Icelandic whaling fleets; landing covertly on the coast of Siberia to film Russian violations of International Whaling Commission rules; blockading the harbor of St. John's, Newfoundland, Canada, to keep the sealing fleet from reaching the seal nursery; and destroying or confiscating miles of Japanese drift nets in the North Pacific Ocean.

Although Watson has been criticized by other members of the environmental movement for the militant style of his tactics, he uncompromisingly refuses to become less aggressive. To Watson and his followers, action is all. "When I look around today, I see only a few who are fighting for the survival of species and the environment," he says. "Oh, there are many who talk about their concern for the Earth—but talk is easy. What is needed is action. . . . If there are whales, elephants, redwoods and ancient forests a century from now, it will be only because a few individuals among nearly six billion on this planet fought for it." Like others on the far edge of environmentalism, Watson takes the long view. "Environmental activists may be a nuisance and a pain in the ass to the established authorities of the present," he wrote in 1993. "However, to the establishment of the future, we will be honored ancestors."

Violence against property to protect nature is sometimes called "ecotage" (a short form of "ecological sabotage"). Another term for it is monkeywrenching, introduced in the 1975 novel *The Monkey Wrench Gang,* whose author, Edward Abbey, a gruff, colorful, and frequently outrageous Western writer and environmentalist, died in 1989. *The Monkey Wrench Gang* stars a radical activist named George Washington Hayduke and his rowdy band of eco-saboteurs, who try to keep the Glen Canyon dam from being built by burning up bulldozers, ripping survey stakes out of the ground, and generally throwing a monkey wrench into the machinery of "progress."

Abbey did not invent monkeywrenching. Back in 1849, in *A Week on the Concord and Merrimack Rivers,* the New England philosopher and nature lover Henry David Thoreau gently wondered what a crowbar would do to a dam he hated—although he never actually picked up the crowbar. A century later, a Massachusetts farmer named Sam Lovejoy was less restrained. He used a crowbar to topple a 550-foot tower that was part of a planned nuclear reactor, then turned himself in to the police. At his trial, he talked of the hazards of nuclear power and the tradition of civil disobedience; then he was set free because the charge against him contained a technical error.

"The Fox" was the best-known eco-saboteur of the 1970s. Operating in Illinois, he took his nickname from the Fox River, polluted by local industrial plants. The Fox stealthily plugged up the illegal drains through which companies poured their wastes into the river and stopped up their chimneys as a protest against air pollution. He posted banners on highway overpasses and wrote letters to the newspapers, naming the polluters. His boldest stunt was entering the corporate headquarters of U.S. Steel disguised as an office painter and dumping 50 pounds of industrial sludge on the carpet. The Fox then disappeared from public view, and his identity remains unknown.

Other, more aggressive eco-saboteurs were on the prowl around the country. One popular activity was cutting down unsightly billboards (especially those that advertised gasoline and chemical products). For two years in the early 1970s, a group of Tucson, Arizona college students calling themselves the Eco-Raiders targeted the real estate developers who, they felt, were turning the region into a vast suburb of tract houses and strip malls. The Eco-Raiders pulled up survey stakes, vandalized unsold houses, and trashed bulldozers and other construction equipment before they were rounded up by the police.

Abbey, who lived in Tucson, incorporated the Eco-Raiders and other Western eco-saboteurs of the early 1970s into his fictional portrait of Hayduke and the monkeywrenchers. Just as fiction draws upon life, however, life sometimes draws upon fiction. *The Monkey Wrench Gang* was one of the inspirations for the founding of Earth First!, the foremost radical environmental group of the 1980s.

The guiding spirit of Earth First! was Dave Foreman. Born in 1946 and raised in an Air Force family, Foreman, like many American boys, dreamed of being a cowboy; later he planned to become a minister. Foreman's father was transferred often, and the family lived in Texas, the Southwest, Bermuda, and the Philippines. The young Foreman was deeply interested in nature and in animals. He devoured books about wildlife and kept a variety of pets, including a large bull snake. As a senior in high school, lonely and miserable in a new town, he hiked in California's Mojave Desert.

Six feet tall and muscular, Foreman became a professional horseshoer in the early 1970s. His introduction to serious environmentalism came at this time, when he got involved with Black Mesa Defense, an attempt to prevent coal mining on a highland sacred to Hopi and Navajo Native Americans. The environmentalists who fought to save Black Mesa employed every tactic from lawsuits to sabotage in their three-year fight, but in the end they failed. Moved to join the environmental struggle, Foreman went to work for the Wilderness Society and eventually became a lobbyist in its Washington, D.C. office, where he tried—often in vain—to convince the Forest Service not to build roads or allow logging and grazing in roadless areas within the nation's wildernesses.

Foreman grew more and more worried about the fate of the wilderness and troubled by what was happening to the environmental movement. Organizations like the Wilderness Society were becoming large and slick. The professional environmentalists on their staffs seemed increasingly remote from the volunteers who were the foot soldiers of the environmental fight—the career conservationists, Foreman has said, seemed "more at home in a yuppie bar than beside the campfire." With their ever-growing staffs and budgets, the "big ten" conservation organizations were becoming too much like corporations and federal agencies, Foreman felt. Worse yet, he believed, their willingness to compromise was making them ineffective.

In 1979, Foreman left the Wilderness Society and the capital. A year or so later, he and four friends went camping in Mexico's Pinacate Desert, and by the time they returned they had hammered out plans for a new environmental movement, Earth First! It would remain loose, unstructured, and unsophisticated (or crude, as some critics were to say). It would be based on respect for whole ecosystems, as urged by Aldo Leopold in *A Sand County Almanac*. Earth First! would use direct action, including civil disobedience, media stunts, and monkeywrenching. But above all, the organization would stay focused on one issue—protecting the wilderness. "We aren't an environmental group," Foreman insisted:

> *Environmental groups worry about health hazards to human beings, they worry about clean air and water for the benefit of people and ask us why we're so wrapped up in something as irrelevant and tangential and elitist as wilderness. Well, I can tell you a wolf or a redwood or a grizzly bear doesn't think that wilderness is elitist. Wilderness is the essence of everything. It's the real world.*

In 1981, soon after founding the Earth First! movement, Foreman and his colleagues staged their first stunt. They climbed to the top of the hated Glen Canyon Dam and unrolled a 300-foot-long sheet of black plastic. From afar, the plastic looked like a huge, widening crack in the dam. Newspapers from coast to coast ran photographs, and Earth First! was off and running. Since then, Earth First! activists have chained themselves to the branches of old-growth redwoods to keep the trees from being cut and blockaded logging roads with their bodies.

Although Earth First! has claimed that it never officially *encouraged* sabotage, it often *discussed* monkeywrenching—also called "night work," ecodefense, ecovandalism, or ecoterrorism, depending upon one's point of view. Foreman and others published monkeywrenching guides with tips on how to pull stakes, booby-trap logging roads, cripple logging and construction equipment, shut down power lines, and remove billboards. The most controversial monkeywrenching act is tree spiking, in which a nail or a large piece of glass or ceramic is inserted into a tree at least 10 feet above the ground. When a spiked tree is cut into boards at the mill, the spike can damage or destroy costly equipment. Warnings that trees have been spiked have halted the sale or logging of many timber stands. However, after a mill worker in California was seriously injured when a band saw exploded upon hitting a spike, Foreman and others declared that tree spiking should be used only after much thought and as a last resort.

Throughout the 1980s, Earth First! grew larger and more diverse, but Foreman remained its chief public spokesperson. Foreman had the rare gift of charisma, an indefinable ability to draw people's attention and inspire their admiration. Bearded, squint-eyed, and tanned, with a Texas accent, clad in tee shirts and jeans, he resembled the cowboys he had dreamed of as a child. Audiences loved him. He urged them to become eco-warriors, saying, "We must place our bodies between the bulldozers and the rain-forest; stand as part of the wilderness in defense of herself; clog the gears of the polluting machine; and with courage, oppose the destruction of life."

Opponents of Earth First! knew that they had to stop Foreman. Agents of the Federal Bureau of Investigation (FBI) infiltrated Foreman's circle and entrapped him in a phony plot to blow up a power line; in 1989, he and four colleagues were arrested on conspiracy charges. In return for a reduced sentence, Foreman agreed not to encourage monkeywrenching in the future. By the time he went to trial, however, Foreman had left Earth First!, feeling that the group had become a squabbling ground for factions that were more concerned with issues such as feminism and social justice than with the wilderness. Returning to his wilderness roots, Foreman and a few colleagues founded the Wild Earth Society, a network of grass-roots groups working to restore and preserve wilderness ecosystems.

Paul Watson, Dave Foreman, and other radical environmentalists share a belief in "deep ecology," an ancient concept that was revitalized in the 1970s by a Norwegian philosopher named Arne Naess. According to Naess, traditional approaches to conservation and environmental protection are based on "shallow ecology." They are merely superficial attempts to cure the symptoms of environmental disorder without treating the underlying disease. Deep ecology, on the other hand, calls for a profound change in the way humans view their relationship with the rest of the world. Instead of taking an anthropocentric ("human-centered") view, deep ecologists see the world as biocentric ("life-centered") or ecocentric ("ecosystem-centered"). To a deep ecologist, *all* living things are of equal value. Humans are neither better nor more important than bison, boll weevils, or bluebirds. The only way in which humans differ from the rest of nature is in their power to destroy it—or to preserve it.

Deep ecologists reject human dominance over nature in favor of harmony with nature. They claim that natural environments and the plants and animals that live in them have a right to exist— not because of their usefulness or attractiveness to humans, but for their own sakes. That right to exist should not be trampled underfoot by humans' lust for material possessions, their rampant population growth, or their desire for endless economic expansion and consumption.

Deep ecology touched a powerful chord in some American environmentalists and has influenced a number of leading ecological thinkers. Yet most people, including most mainstream environmentalists, question the fundamental basis of deep ecology, feeling that it is not only natural but proper to feel that human needs and values are of primary importance. Critics have also been repelled by the extreme statements of a few deep ecologists, who believe that it is urgently necessary to reduce human overpopulation. Some of the deepest of the deep ecologists have suggested that, because food shortages and diseases are nature's way of restoring the balance between populations and their environments, famines and plagues should be allowed to run their course unchecked by medical aid or food supplies. Many people within and outside the environmental movement find such ruthlessness disturbing.

As Dave Foreman and other radical environmentalists have recognized, one of their functions has been to redefine the "mainstream" and the "fringe" of the environmental movement. One decade's fringe is the next decade's mainstream. For example, the Sierra Club was once viewed as a conservationist fringe group, but when Friends of the Earth and other, more radical organizations came along, the Sierra Club started to look moderate and mainstream. Friends of the Earth, in turn, was displaced from the radical edge by Greenpeace, Sea Shepherds, and Earth First! By occupying the farther fringes of environmentalism, these groups have made other environmentalists appear moderate and therefore socially acceptable. The radical groups have also underlined the fact that environmentalism is far from unified. Although environmentalism began with a fairly narrow focus on wilderness preservation, today it is perhaps the most sprawling, diverse, and undefined reform movement ever seen in the United States.

CHAPTER EIGHT NOTES

page 94   "If crazy stunts . . ." *Robert Hunter,* **Warriors of the Rainbow: A Chronicle of the Greenpeace Movement,** p. 252.

page 95   "When I was a teenager . . ." *Paul Watson,* communication to author.

page 96   "When I look around . . ." *Paul Watson,* communication to author.

page 96   "Environmental activists may be . . ." *Paul Watson,* **Earthforce,** p. 113.

page 99   "more at home . . ." *Dave Foreman,* **Confessions of an Eco-Warrior,** p. 203.

page 99   "We aren't . . . Environmental groups . . ." *Dave Foreman, 1987.* Quoted in *Christopher Manes,* **Green Rage: Radical Environmentalism and the Unmaking of Civilization,** p. 72.

page 100   "We must place our bodies . . ." *Dave Foreman,* "It's Time to Return to Our Wilderness Roots," **Environmental Action,** December–January 1984, pp. 24–25.

CHAPTER **Nine**

ENVIRONMENTALISM FOR EVERYONE?

The environmental movement is not a single, unified force. It takes many forms, some of them official and well-organized, others spontaneous and individual. At one end of the spectrum are the large organizations, including the federal agencies that manage resources and enforce environmental rules. Although most environmental activists regard the Environmental Protection Agency, the Forest Service, and the Bureau of Land Management as the enemy, some of the people who work for these agencies are deeply committed to caring for the environment and believe that the most effective way to do so is through agency service.

The mainstream of the environmental movement consists of large organizations such as the Sierra Club, the Wilderness Society, the Audubon Society, the World Wildlife Fund, the Nature Conservancy, the National Wildlife Federation, Greenpeace U.S.A., the Environmental Defense Fund, and others that operate nationally and internationally. Most of these groups started with half a dozen people and a few dollars, but today they have large, full-time professional staffs as well as volunteer forces; some also fund their own research scientists. The big groups now have big budgets and are good at fund-raising, public relations, and enlisting celebrities to support their causes. Their activities tend to cover a broad range of issues, often with a global focus: protecting endangered habitats and species, maintaining the health of the oceans, fighting to save rainforests and old-growth forests, studying global warming and the ozone hole. Because they have large memberships and have been around long enough to become established and familiar, the big groups have had some success in influencing business and government. They are considered the movement's mainstream because they represent the positions of the majority of people who call themselves environmentalists.

Smaller and less organized than the mainstream groups are the local, grass-roots groups: the NIMBYs. Motivated more by immediate fears for the health and safety of their communities than by global concerns, NIMBY groups—some representing areas as small as a city block—have been very effective in dealing with local problems. Sometimes many NIMBYs join together in large, loose networks to share information or to make their voices heard in Congress. Such coalitions among grass-roots activists are likely to increase as computer networking becomes more widespread. Many NIMBY activists also belong to one or more of the large mainstream groups. A fair number of the grass-roots activists, however, are concerned only with a particular local crisis and have no connection to the larger environmental movement.

The radical strain of the environmental movement consists of people whose ideas and beliefs diverge from the mainstream. It includes thinkers like Murray Bookchin and Barry Commoner, who have linked environmental reform to large, revolutionary changes in society, such as a decentralized government or a socialist economic system. It also includes the deep ecologists, who have rejected a human-centered system of values, and groups and individuals who practice monkeywrenching and ecotage.

Millions of people show some degree of concern for the environment in their everyday lives. They recycle. They don't waste water when washing their dishes or their cars. They expose their children to zoos and nature programs. They try to avoid unnecessary driving, and they buy new cars with energy conservation in mind. Perhaps they subscribe to the Sierra Club's magazine or belong to the local chapter of the Audubon Society. These people are not only part of the environmental movement; their quiet actions are its foundation.

Young people are part of the environmental movement— some would say the most important part, since they will deter-

Young environmentalists collect recyclable aluminum beverage cans. Even very young children can be drawn into environmentalism through hands-on activities like this or through their delight in animals. *(S.C. Delaney, Environmental Protection Agency)*

mine the fate of the environment in the future. Hundreds of books, magazines and television shows on environmental themes have been produced specifically for children and teenagers. Many kids have become activists, either with their families and classmates or on their own. Students in elementary and middle schools volunteer for many environmental activities, from beach and park cleanups to fund-raising for local zoos and nature centers. In 1987, high school students helped launch the nationwide McToxics campaign to pressure the McDonald's fast-food corporation into dropping its wasteful and environmentally destructive polystyrene packaging. College and university campuses have been fertile ground for environmental activism since the late 1960s. In 1988, students at the University of North Carolina formed the Student Environmental Action Coalition (SEAC), a network of more than 200 campus organizations around the country; a year later, more than 1,700 people attended SEAC's first national student environmental conference.

The American environmental movement not only takes many forms but embraces a multitude of issues and causes. The traditional core issues of wilderness and wildlife preservation are still central to the movement, although they have become global, concerned with tropical rainforests and African wildlife as well as with Rocky Mountain wilderness and grizzly bears. Wilderness and wildlife preservation are related to the cause that ecologists feel is most urgent: protecting biodiversity, slowing the rate at which species and their habitats are being driven into extinction.

Other issues are related to the health and safety of humans and the rest of the environment. These issues include air and water pollution; the buildup of garbage and trash; and the production, storage, and disposal of hazardous wastes, such as toxic chemicals and radioactive materials. Nuclear safety is a major issue for both the environmental movement and the peace movement. Peace activists tend to oppose nuclear power because of its military potential. Environmentalists debate the advantages and disadvantages of nuclear energy; some feel that it is less destructive to the environment than fossil fuels such as oil and coal, while others point to the hazards of radiation leaks and the problem of what to do with radioactive waste.

The issue of overpopulation lurks beneath the surface of nearly all environmental discussions. Overpopulation is certainly not the sole cause of problems such as wildlife habitat loss, deforestation, or the shrinkage and pollution of groundwater resources, but population pressures make these and other environmental problems increasingly difficult to solve.

The animal-rights movement is independent of the environmental movement and is more concerned with preventing cruelty to and exploitation of individual animals than with the conservation of species. At times, however, environmentalists and animal-rights activists join forces—for example, in battling the trade in exotic wildlife or in exposing the use of endangered species as laboratory animals. Some animal-rights activists have adopted techniques that were pioneered by eco-saboteurs, such as media stunts and monkeywrenching.

A number of environmental issues concern the administration of public lands. The conflict between those who want to preserve national forests and those want to harvest them goes all the way back to the earliest days of the national forest system and is now hotter than ever. Similar battles are being fought over oil drilling in the Arctic National Wildlife Refuge and reef fishing in marine sanctuaries. New conflicts have entered the picture as well. Preservation purists who want to keep the human impact on wilderness areas and public lands to a minimum are fighting challenges by rival users of these lands, such as cross-country motorcyclists and snowmobilers, who claim that they have as much right as hikers to the deserts, forests, and trails.

Women have long been a driving force in the NIMBY movement, especially in antinuclear and antitoxics campaigns. For the most part, they are concerned with health and safety issues, not with the larger issue of women's rights and roles. Since the 1970s, however, a few thinkers have been examining the links between ecology and feminism, which focuses on women's equality with men. The term *ecofeminism* was coined in 1974 to describe this fusion of environmentalism and feminism. Ecofeminism has been explored in such books as Rosemary Ruether's *New Woman, New Earth* (1975), Susan Griffin's *Woman and Nature* (1978), and *Reweaving the World: The Emergence of Ecofeminism* (1990), edited by Irene Diamond and Gloria Feman Orenstein. Many ecofeminists believe that a male view of nature as something to be dominated or exploited is to blame for the current woeful state of the environment; some say that environmental reform requires new social and spiritual values based on qualities such as empathy and cooperation, which they believe to be characteristically female.

Religion and ecology are becoming allies in a movement called *ecotheology* as religious thinkers and members of the clergy begin to regard environmental damage as an insult to the world that God created. Traditional or conservative Christians point to *Genesis* 1:28, in which God tells humans to rule the world and make use of its riches; but the ecotheologians answer with another biblical passage, *Jeremiah* 2:7, in which God says, "I brought you to a fertile country to enjoy its produce and good things; but no sooner had you entered than you defiled my land, and made my heritage detestable."

Father Thomas Berry, a leading ecotheologian, is a Roman Catholic priest who believes that the ecological crisis demands "a new sense of what it means to be human," a new humility about humankind's place in the universe, and a respect for the rest of creation. Such views were once ignored by the officials of the major faiths, but in 1989 Pope John Paul II released a surprising statement outlining the Roman Catholic church's new position on the environment. Declaring that "greed and selfishness, individual and collective, have gone against the order of creation," the pope wrote, "The ecological crisis has assumed such proportions as to be everyone's responsibility." In 1993, the National Religious Partnership for the Environment, a council representing the Jewish, Roman Catholic, Protestant, and Evangelical faiths, began a three-year campaign to make environmental awareness part of religious life for thousands of congregations.

Some religious aid workers are drawn to the ecotheological point of view by witnessing the powerful connections between the environment and social justice. Poverty and human suffering are often closely linked to ecological disasters—in Mali, for example, where overgrazing and population growth have turned grasslands into desert, or in Bangladesh, where floods caused by tree-cutting in the Himalayan foothills have killed people by the hundreds of thousands. Many people outside the religious community also regard environmentalism as part of a broad quest for social, racial, and economic justice.

By the early 1990s, the United States seemed to be getting "greener." Environmentalism had moved into everyday American life. Most communities had recycling centers. Ecological themes were becoming more common in books, newspapers, and magazines. More than a few reporters and writers were devoting themselves to environmental issues. The Society of Environmental Journalists was founded in 1990, and by December of 1993 it had become "the country's fastest-growing journalism organization," with 900 members in the United States and 20 other countries. Television documentaries such as *Nature, Nova, Wild America,* and the productions of the National Geographic and Cousteau societies had found a large audience on public and cable networks. Hollywood had flirted with environmentalism in movies as varied as *Ferngully, the Last Rainforest,* an animated children's film, and *On Deadly Ground,* an action film about oil drilling in Alaska. At least 30 states had added environmental education programs to their public school curricula, and many universities offered programs in environmental studies. Environmental law was one of the fastest-growing fields of legal study; in 1989, the president of the Environmental Law Institute estimated that American government agencies, corporations, law firms and environmental organizations employed 20,000 specialists in environmental law.

But does this "greening" mean that the environmental movement has truly gained strength? Or is America green only on the surface? In many ways, environmentalism has slowed down since the 1970s, and the large national environmental groups have felt the pinch. These organizations grew rapidly in the 1970s and early 1980s, but since the mid-1980s the flow of new members has slowed and operating costs have increased. Some groups, including Greenpeace U.S.A. and the Sierra Club, have had budget crises that forced them to cut back the size of their staffs.

In December 1991, *Outside* magazine's cover story—headlined "The Incredible Shrinking Environmental Movement"—reported on what the magazine's editors called the "backlash against environmentalism." That backlash was fed by the antienvironmental attitudes of the Reagan and Bush presidencies. Environmentalists cheered the election of Bill Clinton in 1992—not because of Clinton's own environmental record, which was poor, but because his running mate was Al Gore, a senator who had publicly committed himself to environmental reform. With the passage of time, however, many leading environmentalists admitted their disappointment that the Clinton administration had not taken a stronger position on environmental issues.

Hard times have hurt the environmental movement. In the 1930s, during the Great Depression, environmental issues took a back seat to economic survival. The same thing has happened, although on a far smaller scale, since U.S. economic growth slowed in the late 1980s. When money is tight, both governments and individuals cut back on the amount they are willing to spend to protect the environment. And when people begin to lose their jobs, particularly in resource-based industries such as logging and mining, environmentalism becomes the enemy. Environmentalists argue that these industries are losing jobs not because of environmental protection laws but because the resources that support them are being used up or abused; for example, salmon fishing is threatened as a livelihood in the Pacific Northwest because the salmon are being wiped out by overfishing, dams, and pollution (mostly sediment draining into rivers from hills that have been logged). Yet when jobs are at stake, it is natural for workers to lash out at the restrictions that prevent them from earning a living, rather than confronting the large, abstract issue of how society uses its resources.

The environment acquired a new enemy in the late 1980s: the Wise Use Movement, a coalition of about 400 antienvironmental groups that are backed by the oil, gas, timber, ranching, mining, and real estate industries. Endorsed by conservative politicians, including former president George Bush and former vice president Dan Quayle, the Wise Use movement argues that environmentalists are unfairly blocking access to the nation's resources and thus costing the American people jobs, new homes, and other desirable things. Two of the leading spokespeople for the movement are Ron Arnold and Alan Gottlieb of the Center for the Defense of Free Enterprise (CDFE). Their book *The Wise Use Agenda* (1988) outlines the movement's goals, which include mining and oil exploration in all national parks, wildernesses, and monuments; the logging of all remaining old-growth forests in the United States; and an end to the protection of endangered plant and animal species.

In the 1950s and 1960s, conservatives used scare tactics to turn Americans against the civil rights movement by painting dramatic pictures of racial turmoil and threats to the white "all-American" way of life. In the same way, the Wise Use Movement stirs up antienvironmental feeling by focusing on the most extreme parts of the environmental movement, the deep ecologists and monkeywrenchers. The shapers of the Wise Use philosophy portray all environmentally concerned citizens as tree-hugging weirdos, mentally ill radicals, or dangerous socialists. "Fear, hate, and revenge," the CDFE's Ron Arnold has admitted, are the basis of Wise Use fund-raising efforts; Arnold has also pointed out that "facts don't really matter. In politics, perception is reality." The creators of the Wise Use Movement like to talk about the coming "ecology wars," in which they and their followers will defend American values, such as the "beleaguered flame of individual liberty" and the "material and spiritual well-being that we free enterprisers cherish."

The Wise Use Movement is about money: economic development versus environmental protection. But the environmental movement has also drawn criticism from scientists and scholars who have questioned the accuracy of its claims and the value of its underlying principles.

Environmental education, particularly in the public schools, has been shown to have some flaws. Many of the books, films, and teacher's guides that schools use have been hurriedly prepared to meet the need for environmental materials for the classroom, and sometimes they contain inaccurate or out-of-date information. In addition, many of these materials are prepared either by environmental groups such as Greenpeace or by corporate interests such as the plastics or oil industry. Both sides claim that their teaching materials are based on science, but educators complain that each side slants its materials toward its own point of view, often leaving the other side of the story out of the picture altogether. For example, many schoolchildren are bombarded with messages about the need to save the rainforest, but few of them are told *why* people are cutting down the forest at such a rapid rate. Teachers say that even very young children can understand concepts such as the desire to obtain farmland or the need for jobs, and that young people should be given more balanced portrayals of environmental issues.

The National Science Teachers Association has also pointed out that many environmental education materials are not only one-sided but oversimplified. Such materials present ecological issues in a right-or-wrong way, failing to teach students that science is often tentative and complex. One example is the controversial issue of global warming. Scientists are still debating whether the Earth's temperature is actually being raised by human activities such as the burning of forests and fossil fuels. Rather than letting students think that global warming is an established "fact," teachers should introduce students to the ongoing debate and let them review the evidence presented by experts who claim that global warming is taking place and compare it with the arguments of those who disagree. In this way, students will learn that environmental science often operates in gray areas of opinion and interpretation, rather than in black and white certainties.

Teachers know that most environmental materials do not do justice to the complexity of the issues. They also realize that those who prepare the materials want to influence children. One Pennsylvania high school teacher showed her students a film about the 1989 *Exxon Valdez* oil spill in Alaska's Prince William Sound. The film, which was produced by the Exxon Corporation, claimed that damage to the Alaskan ecosystem was not severe, but the teacher knew that many scientists would strongly disagree with that claim. "One of the dilemmas that we have," she said, speaking for all environmental educators, "is 'Who do we believe?'"

The same question has been asked about environmental publications aimed at adults. Popular writers on environmental issues have been accused of presenting readers with inaccurate, one-sided, or distorted facts or arguments. Some of these accusations are true; environmental popularizers—like corporate scientists—have sometimes been guilty of careless research or of slanting their arguments to support their own beliefs and interests. Eventually, questions about "bad science" find their way to the places where scientists traditionally evaluate and debate new findings and theories: the scientific journals and associations. The question of whether environmentalists' arguments are one-sided or slanted is battled out in the popular press. In recent years, books such as John Maddox's *The Doomsday Syndrome* (1978), Dixy Lee Ray's *Environmental Overkill* (1993) and Michael Fumento's *Science Under Siege* (1993) have offered alternative interpretations of ecological issues to correct what they call the extremism of the environmental movement.

Environmental writers have also been accused of using scare tactics—that is, of painting an unnecessarily grim picture of environmental disaster in order to frighten people into adopting the measures that environmentalists believe are necessary. Ronald Bailey's *Ecoscam: The False Prophets of Ecological Apocalypse* (1993) and Elizabeth Whelan's *Toxic Terror* (1984) claim that environmentalists knowingly or unknowingly exaggerate ecological dangers and mislead the public.

Some observers have questioned not just the scientific accuracy but also the underlying values of environmentalism. One thoughtful and well-presented criticism of the environmental movement is Charles T. Rubin's *The Green Crusade: Rethinking the*

Roots of Environmentalism (1994). Rubin examines the works of the science popularizers and social theorists who have shaped the contemporary environmental movement, from Rachel Carson to deep ecologist Arne Naess, looking for the moral and political underpinnings of the movement. Rubin claims that environmentalism is based on "anti-human" principles that are hostile to reason, technology, and progress. He also points out that although clean air and safe industries are admirable goals, many environmentalists have envisioned deeper and more radical changes in society, and he warns that with the failure of the "red" idealism of international communism, the "green" idealism of the environmental movement may be the next threat to democracy.

If the environmental movement is to remain effective, it cannot lightly dismiss its critics. Environmentalists must weigh and respond to the arguments against them. They must acknowledge scientific mistakes or biases when these occur, and they must be rigorous in providing the best and most thorough documentation for all claims. Environmentalists should make a special effort to keep the respect of teachers by being even-handed and thoughtful, not manipulative and emotional, when communicating with young people. In addition, environmentalists need to be aware of the movement's history and of their own goals, while recognizing that "environmentalism" covers a lot of territory. No single ecologist, activist, philosopher, or organization can speak for the entire movement.

Many books have been written about the history of the environmental movement, quite apart from the thousands of volumes that deal with environmental and ecological issues. Some environmental histories are biographies of key individuals or chronicles of particular organizations. Other volumes examine the movement in a larger historical context, looking at its origins and its effects. In *A Fierce Green Fire: The American Environmental Movement* (1993), environmental journalist Philip Shabecoff traces the movement's growth from its origins among hunters and preservationists to the present. Robert Gottlieb, an urban planner and author of *Forcing the Spring: The Transformation of the American Environmental Movement* (1993), takes a less traditional view of the movement's origins. Environmentalism, Gottlieb says, springs not only from the wilderness preservationists but also from the activists of the late 19th and early 20th centuries who fought for social betterment through reforms in worker safety and public health.

The American environmental movement reached a milestone in 1990: the 20th anniversary of the first Earth Day. Two hundred million people in 140 countries took part in Earth Day 1990, which the *New York Times* called "the largest grass-roots demonstration in history," involving "more people concerned about a single cause than any other global event in history." But how far had the environmental movement really come in the two decades since the first Earth Day?

Not very far, according to Denis Hayes, who organized Earth Day 1970 and Earth Day 1990. In the April 1990 issue of *Natural History* magazine he examined the state of the world and of the environmental movement and asked, "What went wrong during the last twenty years?" In Hayes's view, the environmental movement had lost much of its momentum since 1970. It had relied too much on government to bring about change; it had failed to form bonds with the poor and with minority groups concerned with environmental justice; and it had not demanded "heroic changes" in the lifestyles and consumption habits of its supporters. Hayes urged environmentalists to confront two vital American and global issues: overpopulation and the soaring military budgets that drain funds away from social and environmental programs. "It will not be possible to build a sustainable society," he said, "without confronting some controversial, emotional issues."

Two years after Earth Day 1990, the largest gathering of world leaders in history met in Rio de Janeiro, Brazil, for the first United Nations Earth Summit—an attempt to bring the nations of the world together to solve environmental problems. The United States lent only weak support to the Summit. American environmentalists were furious that President Bush refused to attend; to many people in the United States and elsewhere, his absence was a sign that the United States took little interest in the world's ecological problems. The Earth Summit produced much talk and thousands of pages of documents, but little in the way of measurable results. However, it did set a pattern for future international efforts, which may be more effective at bringing about environmental reform.

Although leaders of the environmental movement feel that progress has been slow and uneven, the movement *has* changed the way Americans think about the environment. More people than ever before are worried about environmental degradation and hazards. A 1992 survey by an independent research firm found that almost 80 percent of the people surveyed felt that human activities were destroying the environment and threatening human well-being. More than half of those people felt that environmental problems were getting worse. Leaders of the environmental movement welcome this sense of urgency. They would like to turn every concerned citizen into an environmentalist. David Brower of the Earth Island Institute said in 1994, "It's no longer enough to slow the rate at which things get worse. We have to accelerate the rate at which things get better."

CHAPTER NINE NOTES

page 108   "I brought you to a fertile land . . ." *Jeremiah* 2:7, **The Jerusalem Bible.**

page 108   "a new sense . . ." Fr. Thomas Berry. Quoted in *David O'Reilly,* "God's Green Earth," **Philadelphia Inquirer,** March 7, 1993, p. L1.

page 109   "greed and selfishness . . . The ecological crisis . . . " Quoted in *Philip Shabecoff,* **A Fierce Green Fire: The American Environmental Movement,** p. 127.

page 109   "the country's fastest-growing . . ." *Ron Chepesiuk,* "Covering the Environmental Beat," **Editor & Publisher,** December 18, 1993, p. 18.

page 111   "Fear, hate, and revenge . . ." Quoted in *Jon Krakauer,* "Brownfellas," **Outside,** December 1991, p. 114.

page 111   "facts don't really matter . . ." Quoted in *Jon Krakauer,* "Brownfellas," **Outside,** December 1991, p. 72.

page 113   "beleaguered flame . . . material and spiritual well-being . . ." *Ron Arnold,* **Ecology Wars.** Quoted in *Jon Krakauer,* "Brownfellas," **Outside,** December 1991, p. 71.

page 113   "One of the dilemmas . . ." Quoted in *Peter West,* "Skeptics Questioning the Accuracy, Bias of Environmental Education," **Education Week,** June 16, 1993, p. 12.

page 115   "the largest grass-roots . . . more people concerned . . ." *Robert McFadden,* "Millions Join Battle for a Beloved Planet," **New York Times,** April 23, 1990, p. 1.

page 116   "heroic changes" . . . " It will not be possible . . ." *Denis Hayes,* "Earth Day 1990: Threshold of the Green Decade," **Natural History,** April 1990, p. 69.

page 116   "It's no longer enough . . ." Quoted in "Inside the Environmental Groups, 1994," **Outside,** March 1994, p. 66.

E P I L O G U E

Into the 21st Century

What issues will be central to the American environmental movement in the years ahead? Within the United States, major issues are likely to include toxic wastes, deforestation, and energy (oil exploration and drilling versus alternative technologies such as solar energy). On the global scene, American environmentalists will remain concerned with overpopulation, the destruction of tropical rainforests, the protection of Antarctica from commercial exploitation and environmental abuse, and the ongoing debates about global warming and the ozone layer. In addition to the

Two faces of the logging controversy: The death of the forests . . .

. . . and loggers fearful of losing their jobs. One person's environmental crisis is another's economic problem. (*U.S. Department of Agriculture, Forest Service*)

substance of the issues, the environmental movement of the next few decades is likely to be shaped by five important trends.

First, environmentalists will have to take economics into consideration. Only the most radical environmentalists now believe that wilderness and wildlife can be preserved for their own sake, in isolation from human needs. Most now accept the need to combine environmental protection with the most ecologically sound forms of economic growth.

"Sustainable development," a concept that links ecology and economics, is a phrase that will be heard often as environmentalism enters the 21st century. It refers to using resources in a way that allows people to earn a living without destroying the resource base upon which they and the other inhabitants of their ecosystem depend—for example, identifying rainforest products, such as nuts and oils, that can be harvested and marketed without cutting down all the trees. Factories and ranchers will have to include environmental degradation and restoration in their costs of doing business; demands for environmental protection will have to include job retraining and financial aid for people whose livelihoods are affected. The connection between ecology and economics is already being explored in creative ways. Several of the large environmental groups have helped arrange "debt-for-nature" swaps with the Third World, in which countries such as Madagascar or Costa Rica are excused from repaying money they owe to the United States or to the World Bank in exchange for preserving a tract of rainforest. Closer to home, an environmental group in Oregon agreed to buy hay for a rancher in exchange for his forgoing the right to take water from a local river; leaving the water in the river should protect local wildlife.

Second, the NIMBY movement will remain strong. New grass-roots groups will form constantly to combat local problems. In addition, the NIMBY approach—now used mostly by antitoxics and antinuclear activists—will be adopted by wilderness preservationists. A few small, grass-roots organizations have already proved surprisingly effective on wildlife and habitat issues. These include Range Watch, a one-woman project to make video documentaries of grazing damage on public lands in the West, and the Northern Alaska Environmental Center, which watches for violations of environmental laws in Alaska's public lands.

Third, there will be increased cooperation and communication among environmental groups. Large and small groups will band together to make the greatest possible impact on legislators. U.S. and foreign groups will pool information and resources. Computer networks and bulletin boards will become leading meeting grounds for activists around the world.

Fourth, the mainstream groups will form bonds with other social activists as they try to shed the lingering image of environmentalists as elite "tree huggers." Environmental justice will become a major cause for all of the national groups. Women and people of color will gain visibility and importance in the movement, not just as dues-payers and volunteers but as leaders and experts.

Finally, environmentalism will play an increasing role in electoral politics. Candidates will be elected—or defeated—on "green" issues. Gus Speth, a founder of the Natural Resources Defense Council who later headed the federal Council on Environmental Quality, says, "We talk about the greening of technology, the greening of this and the greening of that. We really haven't had a greening of politics in the United States." Environmental journalist Philip Shabecoff, who is optimistic about the future of the movement, believes that the greening of politics may be on the horizon, and that candidates may one day run for major offices on the strength of environmental issues.

On one point everyone agrees, from the mainstream of the movement to its farthest fringe: For the deterioration of the natural world to be halted or reversed, people everywhere will have to make real changes in the way they live, work, eat, travel, play, and think. Action is essential. From the heart of the established order, Al Gore wrote of the importance of believing that what we do today will matter in the future:

For civilization as a whole, the faith that is so essential to restore the balance now missing in our relationship to the earth is the faith that we do have a future. We can believe in that future and work to achieve it and preserve it, or we can whirl blindly on, behaving as if one day there will be no children to inherit our legacy. The choice is ours; the earth is in the balance.

Gore is seconded by eco-enforcer Paul Watson, speaking from the movement's militant fringe, who says, "The generation in the middle of the 20th century fought and many died to protect liberty from tyranny. They are remembered for that. Our generation has a more challenging task—to protect the world from ourselves. We will be remembered for our stand today."

EPILOGUE NOTES

page 121   "We talk about the greening . . ." *Gus Speth.* Quoted in *Philip Shabecoff,* **A Fierce Green Fire: The American Environmental Movement,** p. 279.

page 121   "For civilization as a whole . . ." *Al Gore,* **Earth in the Balance: Ecology and the Human Spirit,** p. 368.

page 122   "The generation in the middle . . ." *Paul Watson,* communication to author.

C H R O N O L O G Y

1492   Columbus reaches the Bahamas; European colonization of the Americas begins

1804–06 The Lewis and Clark expedition opens the way for settlement of the American West

1864   George Perkins Marsh publishes *Man and Nature;* Yosemite Valley becomes a California state park

1872   Congress creates Yellowstone, the first national park in the United States

1890   The U.S. Bureau of the Census announces that the frontier has ceased to exist; Yosemite National Park is established

1892   John Muir and others found the Sierra Club

1905   The National Audubon Society is organized

1908   The Grand Canyon of the Colorado River is made a national monument

1913   Muir and the conservationists lose the battle to preserve the Hetch Hetchy Valley

1916   The National Park Service is organized

1922   The Izaak Walton League is founded

1935   The Wilderness Society is founded by Bob Marshall and others to fight for preservation of primitive natural areas

1936   The National Wildlife Federation is founded to promote wildlife conservation

1949   Aldo Leopold's *A Sand County Almanac* is published

1951   The Nature Conservancy is founded and begins buying tracts of ecologically vital land

1955   Congress passes the first Clean Air Act

1956	Conservationists block the construction of the Echo Park Dam in Dinosaur National Monument
1962	Rachel Carson's book *Silent Spring* is published
1964	Congress passes the Wilderness Preservation Act, which allows areas to be held aside from development and commercial activity
1968	Paul Ehrlich publishes *The Population Bomb*
1969	Friends of the Earth is founded
1970	The first Earth Day takes place in the United States; Congress creates the Environmental Protection Agency (EPA) and passes the National Environmental Policy Act (NEPA), the Occupational Safety and Health Act (OSHA), the Solid Waste Disposal Act, and an amended Clean Air Act; the Natural Resources Defense Council and Zero Population Growth are founded
1971	Greenpeace is organized in Canada
1972	The League of Conservation Voters is founded; Congress passes the Federal Water Pollution Control Act, the Marine Mammal Protection Act, the Ocean Dumping Act, and the Federal Insecticide, Fungicide, and Rodenticide Act (FIFRA)
1973	The Endangered Species Act is passed to protect rare species and habitats
1974	Congress passes the Safe Drinking Water Act
1976	Congress passes the Toxic Substances Control Act (TOSCA) and the Resource Conservation and Recovery Act (RECRA)
1977	Congress rewrites and strengthens laws dealing with clean air and water
1978	Toxic waste contamination is found at Love Canal in Niagara Falls, New York; the Sea Shepherd Conservation Society is formed

1980 Congress passes the Comprehensive Environmental Response, Compensation and Liability Act (CERCLA or Superfund) and the Alaska National Interest Lands Act

1981 Dave Foreman and others found Earth First!; Lois Gibbs organizes the Citizens Clearinghouse for Hazardous Waste

1989 Foreman and three other Earth First! members are arrested by the Federal Bureau of Investigation

1990 Two hundred million people in 140 countries participate in the 20th anniversary of Earth Day

1992 The United Nations Conference on Environment and Development (Earth Summit) is held in Rio de Janeiro, Brazil

FURTHER READING

ABOUT THE ENVIRONMENTAL MOVEMENT

Allen, Thomas B. *Guardian of the Wild: The Story of the National Wildlife Federation.* Bloomington: Indiana University Press, 1987. A description of J. N. Darling and the organization he founded, and of the NWF's disagreements with other environmental and conservation groups.

Bailey, Ronald. *Ecoscam: The False Prophets of Ecological Apocalypse.* New York: St. Martin's Press, 1993. A journalist's argument that prominent environmental scientists and writers have deluded the public.

Berry, Fr. Thomas. *The Dream of Earth.* San Francisco: Sierra Club Books, 1988. Thoughts on religious environmentalism, by a leading ecotheologian.

Bierhorst, John. *The Way of the Earth: Native America and the Environment.* New York: Morrow, 1994. A survey of how Native American cultures have interacted with the land.

Bramwell, Anna. *Ecology in the 20th Century.* New Haven: Yale University Press, 1989. A British scholar's survey of the development of environmentalism into a political force in Europe and the United States.

Brown, Michael, and John May. *The Greenpeace Story.* London: Dorling Kindersley, 1989. The history of Greenpeace from its founding by a group of radical activists to its role among the major environmental organizations.

Cohen, Michael P. *A History of the Sierra Club, 1892–1970.* San Francisco: Sierra Club Books, 1988. A history of one of the oldest and most influential environmental groups.

Cronon, William. *Changes in the Land: Indians, Colonists, and the Ecology of New England* (second edition). New York: Hill and Wang, 1984. A study of the effect of European settlement on the first area of the United States to be extensively colonized.

Diamond, Irene, and Gloria Feman Orenstein (editors). *Reweaving the World: The Emergence of Ecofeminism.* San Francisco: Sierra

Club Books, 1990. Essays about the ecofeminist movement, which links environmentalism with women's rights and roles.

Fox, Stephen. *The American Conservation Movement: John Muir and His Legacy.* Madison: University of Wisconsin Press, 1985. A history of the philosophy and practice of wilderness conservation.

Fumento, Michael. *Science Under Siege: Balancing Technology and the Environment.* New York: William Morrow, 1993. A journalist's review of errors, deceptions and extremes in the environmental movement.

Gottlieb, Robert. *Forcing the Spring: The Transformation of the American Environmental Movement.* Washington, D.C.: Island Press, 1993. A survey of the environmental movement focusing on the links between environmentalism and other social issues such as women's and minority rights.

Lewis, Martin. *Green Delusions: An Environmentalist Critique of Radical Environmentalism.* Durham, N.C.: Duke University Press, 1992. An overview of the contemporary environmental movement that links environmentalism to left-wing, socialistic political philosophy.

Manes, Christopher. *Green Rage: Radical Environmentalism and the Unmaking of Civilization.* Boston: Little, Brown, 1990. A survey of the "deep ecology" philosophy and its effects on environmentalism.

Martel, Ned, and Blan Holman. "Inside the Environmental Groups, 1994." *Outside Magazine,* March 1994, p. 65. A guide to who's who and who's doing what among the environmental organizations.

Martin, Russell. *A Story that Stands Like a Dam: Glen Canyon and the Struggle for the Soul of the West.* New York: Henry Holt, 1989. A detailed look at the fight between conservationists and developers over the Echo Park and Glen Canyon dams.

McHenry, Robert, and Charles Van Doren (editors). *A Documentary History of Conservation in America.* New York: Praeger, 1972. A collection of short excerpts from key environmental writings by authors ranging from Henry David Thoreau and Gifford Pinchot to Isaac Asimov.

Milbrath, Lester. *Environmentalists: Vanguard for a New Society.* Albany: State University of New York Press, 1984. A sociologist's interpretation of the environmental movement as a force for fundamental social change.

Nash, Roderick. *Wilderness and the American Mind.* New Haven, Conn.: Yale University Press, 1967. A look at how the idea of the wilderness has affected American politics, literature and society.

————. *The Rights of Nature: A History of Environmental Ethics.* Madison: University of Wisconsin Press, 1989. A survey of efforts to widen the circle of ethical behavior to include the natural world.

Norwood, Vera. *Made from This Earth: American Women and Nature.* Durham: University of North Carolina Press, 1993. Part of the Gender and American Culture series; a study of women's relationships with the natural world and with the conservation movement.

Outside editors. "The Environmental Year in Review." *Outside,* December 1991, p. 50. A collection of six articles on the successes and shortcomings of environmentalism.

Ray, Dixy Lee. *Environmental Overkill: Whatever Happened to Common Sense?* Washington, D.C.: Regnery Gateway, 1993. A critique of environmental extremism, by a former governor of Washington State and head of the Atomic Energy Commission.

Reisner, Marc. *Cadillac Desert.* New York: Penguin, 1987. A history of the "water wars" of the American West, including the controversy over the Echo Park and Glen Canyon dams.

Rubin, Charles T. *The Green Crusade: Rethinking the Roots of Environmentalism.* New York: Free Press, 1994. A survey of the environmental movement since the 1960s, in which the author argues that environmentalism is based not on scientific evidence of ecological problems but on utopian or totalitarian visions of social reform; contains thorough summaries of other attacks on environmentalism.

Shabecoff, Philip. *A Fierce Green Fire: The American Environmental Movement.* New York: Hill and Wang, 1993. A sympathetic, readable history of conservationism and environmentalism from colonial times to the 1990s, written by the former chief environmental reporter for the *New York Times.*

Strong, Douglas. *Dreamers and Defenders: American Conservationists.* Lincoln: University of Nebraska Press, 1971. An overview of the conservation movement through the activities of key individuals.

Talbot, Allan. *Power along the Hudson: The Storm King Case and the Birth of Environmentalism.* New York: Doubleday, 1972. A detailed examination of a landmark case that brought environmentalism into the courtroom.

Zakin, Susan. *Coyotes and Town Dogs: Earth First! and the Environmental Movement.* New York: Viking, 1993. A sympathetic journalist's detailed, sometimes disturbing account of the personalities and politics of environmentalism's radical wing.

Zeff, Robin L. *Environmental Action Groups.* New York: Chelsea House, 1993. A survey of the formation and activities of the major groups, written for young adults.

LANDMARK ENVIRONMENTAL PUBLICATIONS

Abbey, Edward. *The Monkey Wrench Gang.* Salt Lake City: Dream Garden Press, 1985. Originally published 1975. The novel that introduced Hayduke, the anarchic eco-activist, and spread the notion of guerrilla environmentalism.

Adams, Ansel, and Nancy Newhall. *This Is the American Earth.* San Francisco: Sierra Club Books, 1960. The first in the Sierra Club's handsome series of photo-exhibit books. David Brower claimed that this volume won substantial public support for land protection.

Bookchin, Murray. *Our Synthetic Environment.* New York: Colophon, 1974. An argument that humankind lives in an increasingly artificial, unhealthy environment, divorced from the natural world.

Carson, Rachel. *Silent Spring.* Boston: Houghton Mifflin, 1987. Originally published 1962. The book that called public attention to the dangers of pesticides and paved the way for a new, broad-based environmental consciousness; this 25th anniversary edition has an introduction by Carson's biographer, Paul Brooks.

Commoner, Barry. *The Closing Circle.* New York: Knopf, 1972. An argument that destructive technology and a profit-driven social order are responsible for environmental destruction, written by a biologist and prominent antinuclear activist.

Devall, Bill, and George Sessions. *Deep Ecology: Living As If Nature Mattered.* Salt Lake City: Gibbs, Smith, 1985. The book that introduced the principles of "deep ecology" to American conservationists.

Douglas, Marjory Stoneman. *The Everglades: River of Grass.* New York: Rinehart, 1947. A classic combination of ecological awareness and fine writing, now a key document in the current struggle to save what remains of Florida's Everglades.

Ehrlich, Paul. *The Population Bomb.* New York: Ballantine, 1968. A best-selling prediction of environmental disaster as a result of overpopulation.

Hardin, Garrett. "The Tragedy of the Commons." *Science,* Vol. 162, No. 3859 (1968), p. 1243.

Leopold, Aldo. *A Sand County Almanac.* London and New York: Oxford University Press, 1987. Originally published 1948. A forester's deeply felt appreciation of the natural world and a plea for the growth of a "land ethic" in modern society.

Marshall, Robert. "The Problem of Wilderness." *Scientific American,* February 1930.

Muir, John. *The Eight Wilderness-Discovery Books.* Seattle: Mountaineers, 1992. Includes all of Muir's writings, from *The Mountains of California* (1894) to several volumes based on his journals and published after his death.

Osborn, Fairfield. *Our Plundered Planet.* New York: Random House, 1948. An early warning that population growth would eventually outstrip food production.

BIOGRAPHIES AND AUTOBIOGRAPHIES

Axelrod, Alan, and Charles Phillips. *The Environmentalists: Who's Who in Conservation.* New York: Facts On File, 1993. A substantial biographical dictionary with entries on 600 individuals and organizations from the 18th century to the present.

Brooks, Paul. *The House of Life: Rachel Carson at Work.* Boston: Houghton Mifflin, 1972. An authoritative biography of "the mother of modern environmentalism."

Cohen, Michael P. *The Pathless Way: John Muir and the American Wilderness.* Madison: University of Wisconsin Press, 1984. A discussion of Muir's ideas and how they are related to today's environmental issues.

Foreman, Dave. *Confessions of an Eco-Warrior.* New York: Crown, 1991. A volume that is part autobiography, part manifesto, and part monkeywrenching handbook, by one of the founders of Earth First!

Glover, James M. *A Wilderness Original: The Life of Bob Marshall.* Seattle: The Mountaineers, 1986. A biography of the young man who carried on John Muir's fight to save the wilderness and was the principal founder of the Wilderness Society.

Harlan, Judith. *Sounding the Alarm: A Biography of Rachel Carson.* New York: Macmillan, 1985. Written for middle-school readers.

Henricksson, John. *Rachel Carson: The Environmental Movement.* Brookfield, Conn.: Millbrook Press, 1991. A biography written for young adults.

Keene, Ann T. *Earthkeepers: Observers and Protectors of Nature.* New York: Oxford University Press, 1994. Profiles of 100 naturalists and environmentalists, many of them American, in a reference volume written for young adults.

Meine, Curt. *Aldo Leopold: His Life and Work.* Madison: University of Wisconsin Press, 1988. A biography of the forester who helped found the Wilderness Society and wrote *A Sand County Almanac.*

Miller, Peter. "John Wesley Powell." *National Geographic,* April 1994, p. 89. An article that combines biography with an account of Powell's views on conservation and natural history in the American West.

Naden, Corinne. *John Muir: Saving the Wild.* Boston: Houghton Mifflin, 1992. A biography for younger readers.

Rowell, Galen. "The John Muir Trail: Along the High, Wild Sierra." *National Geographic,* April 1989. A beautifully illustrated article that blends biography with a description of Muir's legacy, by one of the world's foremost mountain photographers.

Turner, Frederick. *Rediscovering America: John Muir in His Time and Ours.* San Francisco: Sierra Club Books, 1985. A thorough biography of Muir, with a discussion of his influence on environmentalism.

Watson, Paul. *Sea Shepherd: My Fight for Whales and Seals.* New York: Norton, 1982. An account of the first few years of the Sea Shepherd Conservation Society, by the organization's founder and a founding member of Greenpeace.

CURRENT ENVIRONMENTAL ISSUES

Ashworth, William. *The Encyclopedia of Environmental Studies.* New York: Facts On File, 1992. Entries cover a wide range of topics, from ecological crises to environmental law; written by a former official of the Sierra Club.

Global Tomorrow Coalition. *The Global Ecology Handbook.* Boston: Beacon Press, 1990. A detailed and reliable collection of information about more than a dozen environmental issues, together with suggestions for those who want to become involved in the environmental movement.

Gore, Al. *Earth in the Balance: Ecology and the Human Spirit.* New York: Penguin, 1992. A wide-ranging summary of brewing environmental disaster and an argument for better stewardship of the planet, by a senator who became vice president in 1992.

Hayes, Denis. "Earth Day 1990: The Threshold of the Green Decade." *Natural History,* April 1990, p. 55. A summary of the lack of progress since the first Earth Day in 1970 and a call to renewed action for the 1990s.

Helvarg, David. *The War Against the Greens: The Wise- Use Movement, the New Right, and Anti-Environmental Violence.* San Francisco: Sierra Club Books, 1994. This account of the backlash against the environmental movement focuses on the corporate underpinnings of the anti-environmental movement and on anti-environmental spokespeople such as former interior secretary James Watt.

McKibben, Bill. *The End of Nature.* New York: Random House, 1989. A short, beautifully written look at humankind's effect on the environment and how the relationship between people and the world is being changed forever.

Naar, Jon. *Design for a Livable Planet*. New York: Harper & Row, 1990. A survey of the world's gravest environmental problems, with suggested actions for individuals and groups as well as information about resources and organizations.

Steger, Will, and Jon Bowermaster. *Saving the Earth: A Citizen's Guide to Environmental Action*. New York: Knopf, 1991. A reference handbook on the most serious problems facing the world's land, air, water, and people, with guidelines for action and information about resources and organizations.

Weiner, Jonathan. *The Next One Hundred Years: Shaping the Fate of Our Living Earth*. New York: Bantam, 1990. A concise and well-written overview of global ecological and population trends, with prescriptions for addressing environmental problems.

A G E N C I E S   A N D
O R G A N I Z A T I O N S

GOVERNMENT AGENCIES

Consumer Product Safety
  Commission
6 World Trade Center
New York, NY 10048
212/264-1125

Department of Agriculture (includes
  National Forest Service)
P.O. Box 2417
Washington, DC 20013
202/447-3760

Department of Energy
1000 Independence Avenue SW
Washington, DC 20585
202/586-5000

Department of the Interior (includes
  Bureau of Land Management,
  Bureau of Wildlife and Fisheries,
  and National Park Service)
18th and C Streets
Washington, DC 20240
202/343-3171

Environmental Protection Agency
401 M Street SW
Washington, DC 20460
202/382-2090

Federal Energy Regulatory
  Commission
825 N. Capitol Street NE
Washington, DC 20426
202/357-8200

NATIONAL ENVIRONMENTAL
ORGANIZATIONS

Citizen's Clearinghouse for
  Hazardous Waste
P.O. Box 6806
Falls Church, VA 22040
703/237-2249

Earth Island Institute
300 Broadway, Suite 28
San Francisco, CA 94133-3312
415/788-3666

Environmental Action
6930 Carroll Avenue, Suite 600
Takoma Park, MD 20912
301/891-1100

Environmental Defense Fund
257 Park Avenue South
New York, NY 10010
212/505-2100

Friends of the Earth
218 D Street SE
Washington, DC 20003
202/544-2600

Greenpeace U.S.A.
1436 U Street NW
Washington, DC 20009
202/462-1177

Izaak Walton League of America
1401 Wilson Blvd, Level B
Arlington, VA 22209
703/528-1818

Kids Against Pollution
275 High Street
Closter, NJ 07624
201/768-1332

Kids STOP (Kids Save the Planet!)
P.O. Box 471
Forest Hills, NY 11375
718/997-7387

League of Conservation Voters
1150 Connecticut Street NW
Washington, DC 20036
202/785-8683

National Audubon Society
950 Third Avenue
New York, NY 10022
212/832-3200

National Wildlife Federation
1400 16th Street NW
Washington, DC 20036
202/797-6800

Natural Resources Defense Council
40 W. 20th Street
New York, NY 10011
212/727-2700

Nature Conservancy
1815 North Lynn Street
Arlington, VA 22209
703/841-5394

Public Citizen/Critical Mass
215 Pennsylvania Avenue SE
Washington, DC 20003
202/546-4996

Sea Shepherd Conservation Society
3107-A Washington Blvd.
Marina del Rey, CA 90292
310/301-7325

Sierra Club
730 Polk Street
San Francisco, CA 94109
415/776-2211

Sierra Club Legal Defense Fund
2044 Fillmore Street
San Francisco, CA 94115
415/567-6100

Union of Concerned Scientists
26 Church Street
Cambridge, MA 02238
617/547-5552

United States Public Interest
  Research Group (USPIRG)
215 Pennsylvania Avenue SE
Washington, DC 20003
202/547-9707

Wilderness Society
900 17th Street NW
Washington, DC 20006-2596
202/833-2300

Worldwatch Institute
1776 Massachusetts Avenue NW
Washington, DC 20036
202/452-1999

World Wildlife Fund
1250 24th Street NW
Washington, DC 20037
202/293-4800

YouthAction
1830 Connecticut Avenue
Washington, DC 20009
202/483-1432

Youth for Environmental Sanity
  (YES)
706 Frederick Street
Santa Cruz, CA 95062
408/459-9344

Zero Population Growth
1400 16th Street NW, Suite 320
Washington, DC 20036
202/332-2200

INDEX

Page numbers in *italic* indicate illustrations.

McKibben, Bill 47
McToxics 106
mining industry 43, 110, 111
   abuses of 21, 37, 71, 98
Monkey Wrench Gang, The (Edward Abbey) 97
monkeywrenching. *See* ecotage
Monticello 9
Moran, Thomas 18
Mount Rainier National Park 29
Muir, John 24, 34, 42, 44, 46, 61, 62, 74
   life of 29–32, *30*
   and Pinchot 35, 36–38
   and Theodore Roosevelt 35–36
Murie, Margaret 47
Murie, Olaus 47
Murray, Gary 86
My First Summer in the Sierra (John Muir) 61

N

Naar, Jon 72
Nader, Ralph 85
Naess, Arne 101, 114
National Audubon Society 35, 61, 77, 79, 81, 88, 104, 105. *See also* Audubon Society
National Cancer Institute 74
National Environmental Policy Act 69
national forests 36, 38, 40, 70, 107–108
National Geographic Society 109
national monuments 29, 36, 111
National Park Service 29, 38, 43, 61
national parks 27–29, 36, 70, 111
National Religious Partnership for the Environment 109
National Science Teachers Association 112
National Wildlife Federation (NWF) 40, 41, 61, 71, 77, 86, 104
National Wildlife Week 41
Native Americans 1–2, 5, 6, 62, 87

economic system of 7, 8
   relationship to natural environment 2, 2–3, 6, 7
   study of, by Powell 15, *16*
Natty Bumppo (Cooper character) 10
Natural History magazine 115
natural resources 32, 36, 40
   as part of public domain 37, 38, 69
   decline of 56, 57, 68, 72, 79, 110–111
Natural Resources Defense Council (NRDC) 81, 121
Nature Conservancy 42, 104
   Parks in Peril program 79
Nature television documentaries 109
Nebraska, exploration of 17
Nelson, Gaylord 66
New Conservationism 60
New Woman, New Earth (Rosemary Ruether) 108
New York Times x, 62, 94, 115
New York Zoological Society 56
New Yorker magazine 51, 53
Newsweek magazine 54
Niagara Falls, as public park 27
Niagara Falls, New York, city of 81–83
NIMBY (Not In My Back Yard) *82,* 85–86, 87–88, 92, 105, 108
   in contrast to mainstream groups 86–87, 88
Nixon, Richard 66, 70
Nolan, Thomas 57
North American Wildlife Conference 41
Northern Alaska Environmental Center 120
Nova television documentaries 109
nuclear energy 59, 76, 79, 107
   activism against 55–56, 68, 81, 84–85, *84,* 86, 88, 97, 108